Understanding and Using dBASE® III (including dBASE® II)

Steven C. Ross

College of Business Administration
Marquette University

West Publishing Company
St. Paul   New York   Los Angeles   San Francisco

Cover Design: Bob Anderson, Computer Arts, Inc.

dBASE®III (dBASE®II)
dBASE is a registered trademark of Ashton-Tate.
Screens are reprinted with the permission of Ashton-Tate.

COPYRIGHT © 1986 by WEST PUBLISHING COMPANY
50 West Kellogg Boulevard
P.O. Box 64526
St. Paul, MN 55164-1003

Printed in the United States of America

Library of Congress Cataloging-in-Publication Data

Ross, Steven C.
  Understanding and using dBase III.

  Includes indexes.
  1. Data base management. 2. dBASE III (Computer program)
  3. dBASE II (Computer program) I. Title.
QA76.9.D3R72 1986   005.75'65   85-24678
ISBN 0-314-96211-5

46,670

CONTENTS

PART 1   FUNDAMENTAL DATA BASE OPERATIONS   1

UNIT 1   THE DATA BASE CONCEPT   3

Data Base System Terminology   3
Data Base System Example   4
Data Base System Design   7

UNIT 2   THE dBASE ENVIRONMENT   11

The dBASE Diskettes   11
The dBASE Keyboard   12
Startup Procedure   15
    Floppy Disk Systems   16
    Hard Disk Systems   18

UNIT 3   DATA FILE CREATION   21

Commanding dBASE   22
Quitting   22
Creating a Data File   23
Data Entry   27
    Opening a File   27
    Adding Data to a File   27
Saving Your Work   28
Viewing the Data in a Data File   29
Editing Data   30
Backup   31

APPLICATION A -- CHEZ JACQUES (I)   37

PART 2 INTERMEDIATE DATA BASE OPERATIONS   41

UNIT 4 CONDITIONS AND EXPRESSIONS   43

Logical Conditions vs. Computed Expressions   44
The Calculator   44
Operators   44
Functions   48
Constrained Lists   51

UNIT 5 SUMMARY STATISTICS   55

Counts   55
Sums   56
Averages   56
Examples   56

UNIT 6 DATA FILE ORDER AND SEARCH   61

Ordering the Data in a File   62
Searching through a File   66

APPLICATION B -- CHEZ JACQUES (II)   73

UNIT 7 OPERATING PARAMETERS AND DISK FILES   75

Operating Parameters   76
 Displaying Parameters   76
 Changing Parameters   76
Disk Files   80
Output to Other Applications Software   82
Input from Other Applications Software   83

UNIT 8 DATA FILE CHANGES   87

Adding Data from Another Data File   88
Changing Data in Existing Records   88
 Systematic Changes   88
 Unsystematic Changes   89
Deleting Entire Records   90
Modifying the Structure of a Data File   94
 Modifying the Structure of a dBASE III File   94
 Modifying the Structure of a dBASE II File   95

APPLICATION C -- MILWAUKEE BANKS   99

UNIT 9 REPORT GENERATION   105

General Considerations   105
Creating the Report Format in dBASE III   107

Producing the Report in dBASE III   112
Report Generation in dBASE II   113

UNIT 10 LABEL GENERATION   119

General Considerations   119
Creating the Label Format   121
Producing the Labels   123

APPLICATION D -- ED AND BRUCE SPECIALTIES (I)   127

PART 3 ADVANCED DATA BASE OPERATIONS   129

UNIT 11 MEMORY VARIABLES   131

Creating Memory Variables   132
Managing Memory Variables   134
Using Memory Variables   136

UNIT 12 COMMAND FILE CREATION AND PROGRAM FLOW   141

Command Files vs. Immediate Mode   142
File and Record Functions   142
Creating Command Files   143
Commands to Control Program Flow   144
    Starting a Program   144
    The Loop   145
    Skipping through a File   146
    Conditional Operations   146
    Exiting the Program   148

UNIT 13 INPUT, OUTPUT, AND POSITIONING   151

Moving about in a Data File   152
Commands for Data Input   153
    Input to a Numeric Variable   153
    Input to a Character Variable   154
    Input of a One-character Response   154
Commands for Output to the User   154
    Output of a Field or Variable   154
    Output of a Block of Text   155
    Output on a New Screen or Page   155
Commands for Output to the Data File   156
Set Commands which Affect Command File Output   157

UNIT 14 CUSTOM INPUT AND OUTPUT FORMS   161

Full Screen Addressing   162
    Full Screen Output   162
    Output Device   163
    Full Screen Input   163
    Combining Output and Input   164
    Erasing Part of the Screen   164
    Changing the Default Screen Format 165

APPLICATION E -- ED AND BRUCE SPECIALTIES (II)   169

UNIT 15 MULTIPLE FILES   173

Opening Multiple Files   174
Aliases and Prefixes   175
    In dBASE III   175
    In dBASE II   175
Multiple File Operations   176

UNIT 16 RELATIONAL DATA BASE OPERATIONS   181

Concepts of Relational Operations   181
    Relation Defined   182
    Types of Relations   182
Establishing Relations   183
Using Relations   184
    Computing   184
    Reporting   185
    Listing   185

UNIT 17 OTHER MULTIPLE FILE OPERATIONS   189

Updating a Data File   190
Creation of a File of Relations   190
Creation of a File of Subtotals   191

APPLICATION F -- CHEZ JACQUES (III)   195

APPENDIX A -- GETTING STARTED ON YOUR MICROCOMPUTER   A-1

APPENDIX B -- ANSWERS   B-1

INDEX   I-1

PUBLISHER'S NOTE

This book is part of THE MICROCOMPUTING SERIES. As such it is an endeavor unique both to West Educational Publishing and to the College Publishing Industry as a whole.

We are "breaking this new ground" because in talking with educators across the country, we found several different needs not easily met by just one publication. Those needs are:

1. To teach the principles or concepts of microcomputer use independent of running specific software programs,
2. To teach the skills of specific application software programs, and
3. To create a microcomputer curriculum flexible enough to handle changes in technology or courses with a minimum of change in the teaching materials used.

THE MICROCOMPUTING SERIES is an innovative attempt to meet those needs by closely integrating a machine independent overview of microcomputers (the core text) with a series of inexpensive, software specific, "hands on" workbooks. Although each text in the series can be used independently, they become especially effective when used together to provide both an understanding of how microcomputers work as well as experience using popular software packages.

We hope THE MICROCOMPUTING SERIES fits your needs and the needs of your students, and that you will adopt one or more of its components for use in your classes. We are also interested in hearing your reaction and suggestions concerning our series and encourage you to share your ideas with us through:

West Publishing Company
College Division
50 W. Kellogg Blvd.
P.O. Box 43526
St. Paul, MN 55164

ABOUT THE AUTHORS

Steven C. Ross holds a B.S. degree in History from Oregon State University and M.S. and Ph.D. degrees in Business Administration from The University of Utah. Currently he is an Assistant Professor of Management at Marquette University in Milwaukee, Wisconsin. At Marquette, he has been responsible for the introduction of microcomputers into the primary computer course and for the integration of computer applications throughout the curriculum. Dr. Ross also consults with businesses of all sizes to integrate microcomputers into the managerial operations of those organizations. His teaching and consulting experiences have provided ample material for this book.

PREFACE

With a true view all the data harmonize,
but with a false one the facts soon clash.
Aristotle, *Ethics*

Understanding and Using dBASE III (Including dBASE II) is about the management of data on personal computers, more specifically, the use of the popular programs dBASE III and dBASE II. Data are the lifeblood of an organization, and the business student and professional must know how to manage data if he or she is to be a successful manager. Not only are the dBASE packages powerful data managers in their own right, and they are also good tools for learning about data management concepts in general.

WHY THIS BOOK?

There are many books available that discuss dBASE II and III. Why then would anyone write another book? I decided to do so because both my students and my colleagues at several universities desired a book tailored to the way personal computing is taught at the college and professional level. We felt that there was no book which was designed for use in academic or workshop settings. We felt a need for a book which would present concepts and skills as well as provide activities, applications, and questions for practice and teaching purposes. *Understanding and Using dBASE III (Including dBASE II)* is such a book.

This book is designed to support the efforts of the instructor by providing the essential facets of the software combined with activities and exercises designed to reinforce and evaluate the student's learning experience. Examples are drawn from the fields of business administration and economics to illustrate how the software may be used in other course work and in the daily tasks performed by business professionals. The instructor's manual provides supplementary materials and suggestions for integrating this book with other course materials.

This book serves a different role than the reference manuals furnished with the dBASE software. These manuals are quite comprehensive, but often are difficult to read and fail to provide adequate examples. This book is designed for instruction in fundamental, intermediate, and advanced operations, supported with substantial reference material. When more detailed information is required, the user will have a significant foundation.

Finally, *Understanding and Using dBASE III (Including dBASE II)* serves as a member of **The Microcomputing Series** published by West Publishing Co. It may be used alone, in combination with other books in the series (listed on the back cover), or tc supplement any other book in a course where a knowledge of dBASE II or III is required.

HOW TO USE THIS BOOK

You should complete the first four units in the order presented. With that background, the material in the remainder of the book may be covered in the order which suits you best. The more work you do on the computer, the better you will learn the topics. As a minimum, you should complete the Guided Activities with each unit. I strongly encourage you to work through the Applications Exercises also. Each activity and exercise is designed to illustrate points made in the previous units, and many contain additional material which is best presented during a computer session.

Each unit includes

Learning Objectives: the knowledge and skills addressed in the unit.

Important Commands: the commands to be covered, which will later serve as a quick reference to the contents of the unit.

Computer Screens: full screen figures depicting the steps and results of most commands.

Guided Activity: a step by step, hands on illustration of the operations discussed in the unit. The activities contain Checkpoints, which ask you questions as you work to further develop your knowledge and skill level. The answers to the Checkpoints are found in Appendix B.

Review Questions: designed to test your understanding of the material presented. The answers to selected review questions are contained in Appendix B.

Documentation Research: exercises which require you to use the software publisher's documentation to learn more about the commands and functions discussed in the unit.

Additional features of *Understanding and Using dBASE III (Including dBASE II)* are

Application Exercises: six exercises spread throughout the book which provide additional practice using the material presented. These are designed to be more challenging than the Guided Activities.

Getting Started on Your Microcomputer: this Appendix is provided as a quick reference for those who need a refresher or minimal reference for the computer hardware and the disk operating system.

Two Indexes: Symbols Index and Alphabetic Index designed to allow you to quickly locate the relevant information.

Keyboard Diagram and Quick Reference: at the back of the book, where you can easily refer to them.

Data Disk: a disk available to instructors which contains both student files (i.e., files needed as input for the Guided Activities and Applications) and instructor files (i.e., solutions to Guided Activities and Applications and files for tests). If you need additional information about this data disk, a demonstration data disk is available. The demonstration data disk includes one unit (chapter) from each of the software workbooks. If you wish to request a copy, please write to: College Department, West Publishing Company, 50 West Kellogg Boulevard, P.O. Box 64526, St. Paul, MN 55164-1003, or contact your West sales representative.

A NOTE OF THANKS. . .

to my father, who taught me the importance of organization and management of data;

to my friends at the insurance company and the magazine publishing company, who motivated me to learn the virtues and the vices of dBASE III and dBASE II;

to the 1000 Marquette students who have used this book in various versions in the past two years, and to my colleagues Bob Armacost, Dick Penlesky, and Joe Fox who asked many critical questions;

to Rich Wohl, Tim Reedy, and Sharon Walrath of West Publishing who guided me in the development of a presentable manuscript;

to the reviewers, Eileen Bechtold Dlugoss of Cuyahoga Community College, Arthur Strunk of Queensborough Community College, and Kathleen Tesker of St. Louis Community College, who made many helpful comments; and

to Meredith, Kelly, and Shannon, who have been most understanding and supportive as I worked on this project.

I hope each of you is pleased with the final product.

If flaws remain, 'tis mine the blame.

S.C.R.
Milwaukee
December, 1985

1 FUNDAMENTAL DATA BASE OPERATIONS

This is the first of three parts in this manual. In this part, we cover fundamental information which you must know to operate dBASE III and dBASE II and which will allow you to construct useful data bases. We will discuss the diskettes which are a part of the dBASE package, how dBASE uses the keyboard, the screen display, and the data base concept.

With that background, we will learn how to create a data base file, how to enter data into that file, how to view the information in the file, how to edit the information in the file, and how to change the structure of the file.

The exercise at the end of this part will guide you through the development of a simple data base. At the conclusion of the exercise, you will have a good introduction to working with dBASE III and dBASE II. The remainder of the manual will prepare you for more sophisticated tasks.

Which version of dBASE are you using? dBASE III offers more functions, but is more expensive, requires more computer memory, and is more easily damaged. dBASE II offers fewer functions, but costs less and is less easily damaged. Much of what is written here applies to both programs, but there are some differences and there are some things that dBASE II does not do. To further complicate matters, there are different versions of both programs, and each of the versions has its own peculiar characteristics.

The major difference between version 1.0 and version 1.1 of dBASE III is the startup procedure, which will be discussed in Unit 2. The other differences between the versions are related to commands which are not presented in this manual.

The differences among the versions of dBASE II are more substantial. As you read through this manual, you will occasionally see the phrase "not available in all versions of dBASE II" which means exactly that -- later versions of dBASE II have incorporated many of the features of dBASE III, but you may be using an earlier version and the command is not available. Unless your instructor advises you otherwise, the best course of action is to try a particular command. It will either work as described in this manual, or dBASE II will inform you that the command is not available.

This manual assumes that you are using dBASE III unless otherwise noted, and you will be alerted, via footnotes, to features that work differently or not at all in dBASE II.

Compatibility between the Versions. Although most commands and concepts are the same in dBASE II and dBASE III, the data files, programs, and indexes created under one system may not be used directly by the other. You must use data files, programs, and indexes created for or by the proper version of dBASE.

If you have been using one version of dBASE and change to the other, you may be able to save most of your work. Ashton-Tate provides a program called dCONVERT with the dBASE III package that will convert dBASE II data files and programs to equivalent dBASE III files. In some cases, dCONVERT may be able to make a dBASE III file into a dBASE II file, but this is not always possible. The conversion from dBASE II programs to dBASE III programs works fairly well, but you must do some editing to insure the validity of your program. There is no utility provided to convert dBASE III programs to dBASE II.

Unit

1

THE DATA BASE CONCEPT

This unit is an intellectual exercise only -- no computer is needed! In this unit we will discuss the terminology of data base management and important factors to consider before you sit down at the computer to begin creating a data base system. This discussion is intended as an elementary introduction to data base design, for a more thorough treatment of the topic, ask your instructor to recommend additional references.

LEARNING OBJECTIVES

1. At the completion of this unit you should know

   a. the definitions of data base management terms,

   b. important considerations before you begin to create a data base system.

2. At the completion of this unit you should be able to describe a simple data base system on paper.

DATA BASE SYSTEM TERMINOLOGY

Since the language of data base management is probably new to you, this section contains brief definitions of some terms, which will be illustrated in the following section.

A **Data Base Management System** (DBMS) is a package of computer programs and documentation that lets you establish and use a data base. The dBASE II and III packages are popular personal computer DBMSs.

A **Data Base** is a collection of interrelated data; the complete collection of data, pointers, tables, indexes, dictionaries, and so forth.

A **Table** is a part of a data base; similar to a two-dimensional table in which the rows are records and the columns are fields; usually stored on a disk as a file. In dBASE, a .DBF file plus associated .NDX files.

A **File** is a collection of data on disk accessed by a unique name; generally a sequence of records of identical format; may contain data, an index, screen format, or report format.

A **Record** is a group of related fields of information treated as a unit -- the "rows" of a table are usually analogous to a record.

The **Fields** of a record contain the data items. You might think of a field as being the location in a record where a data item is stored. A field has certain characteristics such as length and data type (e.g., number, character, date, memo and logical types are found in dBASE III). Fields correspond to "columns" in tables.

A **Byte** is usually one character, letter, number or symbol. Field width is measured in bytes.

The **Data Dictionary** contains a full description of the fields in a data base or a table; describes the relationships among various fields.

An **Index** contains a table of record numbers, called pointers, which are arranged to permit the rapid location of a particular record.

The **Key** is a unique identifier for each record; may be a single field or a group of fields.

DATA BASE SYSTEM EXAMPLE

With those definitions as a basis, it may be worthwhile to consider an example of a data base. Assume for the moment that you are the operator of a fast food restaurant. In your restaurant, you combine raw materials (hamburger patties, buns, lettuce, ice cream, etc.) to produce finished goods (hamburgers, milk shakes, etc.).

Like many manufacturers, you are concerned about your inventory of raw materials. You want to minimize the amount of raw materials on hand because keeping inventory is expensive. You are also worried about spoilage. Before you started using a computer, you kept your inventory on index cards that looked like Figure 1-1.

As a first step in data base development, you transferred your inventory data to a sheet of paper with a result that looked like Table 1-1. Many of the key data base concepts can be illustrated by considering the example in Table 1-1.

Each character in each entry in the table occupies one *Byte*. For instance, each of the date entries is eight (8) bytes wide. When designing a data base, you need to know the maximum width in bytes of the entries in a given field.

```
┌─────────────────────────────────────────────────────────────┐
│                                                             │
│   Stock Number    0014                                      │
│                                                             │
│   Description     12 oz. cup                                │
│                                                             │
│   Cost Each       0.03                                      │
│                                                             │
│   Quantity on Hand    300                                   │
│                                                             │
│   Date of Last Order  10/4/85                               │
│                                                             │
│                                                             │
└─────────────────────────────────────────────────────────────┘
```

FIGURE 1-1 Inventory Card

TABLE 1-1 The Inventory in Tabular Form

Stock Number	Description	Unit Cost	Quantity on Hand	Date of Last Order
0014	12 oz. cup	0.03	300	10/04/85
0015	16 oz. cup	0.05	400	09/28/85
0018	4 oz. fry pack	0.02	332	10/19/85
0019	6 oz. fry pack	0.03	500	10/15/85
0013	8 oz. cup	0.02	600	10/06/85
0011	Coca Cola (oz.)	0.05	800	10/13/85
0012	Sprite (oz.)	0.05	700	10/12/85
0001	all-beef patty	0.10	100	10/01/85
0016	apple pie	0.16	346	08/15/85
0009	catsup (oz.)	0.04	386	10/10/85
0006	ch. onion (oz.)	0.06	876	10/10/85
0004	cheese slice	0.02	255	10/09/85
0017	cherry pie	0.14	200	09/19/85
0010	fren. fry (oz.)	0.01	999	10/12/85
0003	lettuce leaf	0.01	90	10/03/85
0005	pickle slice	0.03	900	09/15/85
0008	regular bun	0.10	200	10/03/85
0007	sesame seed bun	0.12	400	10/08/85
0002	sp. sauce (oz.)	0.01	400	09/30/85

Each entry on the card and each column in the table is called a *Field*. Notice that the type of data is consistent as you read down the column: either numbers, text, or date data. Fields are identified by *Field Names* such as Stock Number, Description, Unit Cost, Quantity on Hand, and Date of Last Order. (dBASE will require us to use shorter names than these illustrations.) As you design a database, consider the types of information you will want to keep as a start toward field definition.

Each card is a separate *Record*. Reading across the rows of the table, we also see what a record is -- a group of related fields of information treated as a unit. Read across the top row, 0014, 12 oz. cup, 0.03, 300, and 10/04/85 are all related to each other: we have 300 12 oz. cups which cost 3 cents each and were last ordered on October 4th. We will need one record for each unique unit, and we must make sure that the data base system we use has sufficient capacity.

All this information is stored in a *Data File*. Without a computer, a file is typically a box of index cards or a manila folder in a cabinet. With a computer, a file is a portion of the disk with unique name. At this point, we may want to start thinking of appropriate filenames for our data files.

The Stock Number field is a *Key* field -- a number or text string which is unique for each record. If our inventory was large, we would build an *Index File*, a table which would allow us to rapidly locate a particular record once we know its key number. As you become more familiar with how your data are arranged, consider how you will want to search for items (e.g., by stock number, perhaps also by description).

The data file, along with index files such as the Stock Number index discussed above, is a *Table*.

We might have other databases, such as a list of suppliers and a list of the items we sell (the menu). Collectively these databases comprise the *Data Base* of the business. Recall that the data base is a collection of interrelated data.

Finally, the *Data Base Management System* is the method by which we manage all this data. Before computers, people used an amazing collection of colored index cards, notes to themselves, and Mrs. MacNamara to keep track of their information. While no computer will ever replace Mrs. MacNamara, a DBMS such as dBASE III or dBASE II does enhance your ability to manage large amounts of data. But dBASE needs your help to manage data, which is what the remainder of this book is about.

Capacity Considerations. Several aspects of DBMS capacity are important. First, the DBMS must allow enough fields to accommodate our needs (see Table 1-2 for a summary of dBASE capacity constraints). Second, the DBMS will impose a certain maximum number of bytes per record. Third, the DBMS must be capable of maintaining the required number of records. Finally, the DBMS will impose a limit on how many databases may be in use at one time. Many applications are be possible using dBASE II, and many more with dBASE III.

TABLE 1-2 dBASE Capacity Constraints

	dBASE II	dBASE III
number of fields	32	128
bytes per record	1000	4000
number of records	65,535	over a billion
number of open databases	2	10

The specific computer system may also impose capacity limitations. A standard IBM PC disk drive will hold about 360,000 bytes of data, which is less than the maximum capacity of a dBASE II data file. Personal computers with hard disks have much more capacity, however, and most organizations maintaining data base systems will use these machines to store their data.

DATA BASE SYSTEM DESIGN

Designing a good data base system is a lot like writing a good newspaper story: who, what, when, where, why, and how. The questions are generally asked in a different order, however.

The most important question is *why*? (Ignoring the possibility that your teacher has provided the why ...) If you have all your important information on a 3x5 card, then you probably do not need to spend $4000 on a computer and DBMS to manage that information. On the other hand, a DBMS will help you if you have a lot of items (i.e., records), several elements of information for each item (i.e., fields), changing attributes which must be accounted for, multiple repetitive computations that you perform, or the need to rapidly locate a given item.

If you start your design process by listing the whys, then you will have a useful guide as you build the elements to manage the data. Be prepared for your list of whys to expand, however, as you realize the potential of your system.

What is really two questions. What data do you have to put into the system, and what output do you want from the system? *What data* is needed in the system will be determined to a large extent by *what output* which is in turn a derivative of *why*.

Sometimes the desired output will be a list, such as a set of mailing labels, sometimes the desired output will be a single item, such as the magazine that certain people regularly read. For instance, if you are a salesperson and wish to have a data base which will provide you with a list of potentially good customers, then you will need data which defines customer goodness (e.g., income, age, previous purchases) as well as data which will enable you to contact the customer (e.g., address, publications normally read).

Timing is important. *When* will the output be required, and when will the data be updated? If you need daily lists, then you need to update data daily. You may have a system which can collect data continuously, such as a computerized cash register, or your input may be based on periodic reports from others, such as monthly sales reports. Update as often as possible, and at least as often as you expect to extract useful data.

Now is a good time to ask *where* the data will come from? Do you have or can you collect the necessary data using current organizational resources, or must you buy the data from elsewhere. The salesperson may have a record of previous purchases and address, but may not know the customers' income or age.

Now you are ready to address *how* the computer will provide the output given the available data. Are there calculations which need to be made? Are there decisions which must be made? Are there criteria for selection? Must the output be sorted in a particular order? Must the data be summarized? Our salesperson may want mailing labels, sorted in Zip code order, of all persons who have made purchases in the past two years, whose household income is more that $20,000. He or she wants to avoid sending more than one copy to a household, so duplicate addresses must be avoided.

One of the more challenging facets of data base design will be forging the link between input and output, the how. While you are in this phase, you should make notes as to how you would do the job by hand. For instance, how would you eliminate duplicate addresses if you had a pile of index cards containing names and addresses?

Finally, you must decide *who* will build the system -- who will write the programs and who will input the data -- and, once the data base is established, who will be responsible for maintaining it -- adding, deleting, or changing data and insuring that the programs continue to function as required. Do not treat this question lightly, maintenance of data is a critical, but usually dull task.

Once you have answered the why, what, when, where, how, and who questions, you are ready to proceed with data base development.

REVIEW QUESTIONS

The answers to questions marked by an asterisk may be found in Appendix B.

1. Define the following terms:

    a. Data Base Management System

    b. Key

    c. Index

    d. Field

    e. Record

    f. Byte

2. What is the difference between a data base and a table?

3. What is the difference between a field and a record?

*4. If each field were 10 bytes wide, what would be the maximum number of fields in a dBASE II record? ... a dBASE III record?

5. Consider the example in Table 1-1. What is the minimum width in bytes necessary for each of the following fields:

    *a. Stock Number

    b. Description

*c. Unit Cost

*d. Quantity on Hand

e. Last Order Date

6. Put yourself in the position of the restaurant manager discussed in this unit. Using why, what, when, where, how, and who, describe a useful data base system. Be creative!

Unit

2 THE dBASE ENVIRONMENT

Before the fun of data base management can begin, we must know how which disks to use, how to start the program, and how dBASE uses the keyboard.

LEARNING OBJECTIVES

1. At the completion of this unit you should know

    a. the use of the dBASE disks,

    b. how dBASE III uses the keyboard.

2. At the completion of this unit you should be able to load the dBASE III program.

IMPORTANT COMMANDS

DBASE

THE dBASE DISKETTES

dBASE III, version 1.0

dBASE III version 1.0 comes with three diskettes, and your organization must supply a fourth diskette with a special version of the Disk Operating System. The most important dBASE disk is the System Disk -- which contains the dBASE III program. This system disk contains the entire dBASE III program and is all you need for most operations. A second copy of the System Disk is labeled the System Disk (Backup Copy), which is usually removed and stored in a safe place.

The third dBASE III disk is the Sample Programs and Utilities Disk. As you might expect, this contains sample programs and data files, as well as ancillary programs. You will not need this disk for the material discussed in this manual, but will need it if you decide to do the tutorial in the dBASE manual.

The fourth disk is supplied by your organization. It must contain the Disk Operating System (MS-DOS or PC-DOS) and a special configuration file placed on the disk by whomever is in charge of the software. This file is called CONFIG.SYS, and allows 20 files and 24 buffers.

These disks are used as noted in the "Startup Procedure" section.

dBASE III, version 1.1

dBASE III version 1.1 comes with four diskettes. The two most important disks are the System Disk #1 and System Disk #2 -- which contain the dBASE III program. These disks are all you need for most operations. A second copy of the System Disk #1 is labeled the System Disk #1 (Backup Copy), which is usually removed and stored in a safe place.

The fourth dBASE III disk is the Sample Programs and Utilities Disk. As you might expect, this contains sample programs and data files, as well as ancillary programs. You will not need this disk for the material discussed in this manual, but will need it if you decide to do the tutorial in the dBASE manual.

Your organization must put the Disk Operating System (MS-DOS or PC-DOS) and a special configuration file on System Disk #1, which will allow you to use that disk to start the computer.

These disks are used as noted in the "Startup Procedure" section.

dBASE II

In most cases, your organization will create one disk which contains the Disk Operating System, the dBASE II program, and any other files needed. While dBASE III is copy protected, dBASE II is not and organizations have greater flexibility in how they configure the dBASE II software.

THE dBASE KEYBOARD

The IBM and other personal computers have over 80 keys, about 40 more than most typewriters. Many of the "extra" keys have symbols or mnemonics rather than characters. To minimize confusion, the following conventions will be used:

Keys with multiple character names will have those names spelled out, usually followed by the word "key":

F1 key
Home key

Del key

Keys with symbols only will have the key name enclosed in <> signs:

<TAB>	gray key just below Esc key
<SHIFT>	gray keys: one between Ctrl and Alt keys, the other just above Caps Lock key
<BACKSPACE>	gray key at top of keyboard
<CR>	gray key between <BACKSPACE> and PrtSc keys
<ARROW KEYS>	white keys on right of keyboard -- also called <UP>, <LEFT>, <DOWN>, and <RIGHT> -- note that <LEFT> and <BACKSPACE> are two different keys and that they do different things.

Keys which yield a single character (such as Aa, $4, and >.) are represented in plain text, assuming that you know when to use the <SHIFT> key:

A4>

Function Keys

These are gray keys on the left side of the keyboard. Two discussed here, the remainder are presented as appropriate throughout this manual.

F1   starts you through a series of Help screens. When you have had enough Help, press the Esc key to get back to the dBASE command prompt.

F2   starts you into the dBASE III Assistant, which is a "command-building" support function not discussed in this manual, and not available in dBASE II.

TABLE 2-1 Function Key Assignments

dBASE III

F1	Help;	F2	Assist;
F3	List;	F4	Dir;
F5	Display Structure;	F6	Display Status;
F7	Display Memory;	F8	Display;
F9	Append;	F10	Edit;

dBASE II

F1	Help;	F2	Disp;
F3	List;	F4	List Files;
F5	List Stru;	F6	List Status;
F7	List Memo;	F8	Create;
F9	Append;	F10	Edit #;

The other function keys will be discussed as needed in later units. See Table 2-1 for a complete list. These keys are not supported by some versions of dBASE II -- ask your instructor if your version of dBASE II does support function keys.

Ctrl-key Combinations

Most people know how to use the <SHIFT> key on a typewriter to produce a capital letter: hold down the <SHIFT> while pressing the letter key. On a computer, the Ctrl and Alt keys work like the <SHIFT> key. To type Ctrl-M, hold down the Ctrl key and press M. In the lists below, a Ctrl-key combination is indicated by preceding the letter with a circumflex:

　　　^N = Ctrl-N

Full-Screen Operations

Many dBASE operations are in "Full Screen" mode, where you are allowed to move the cursor over all or a part of the screen using the keys discussed below. Data input, report creation, and command file creation all operate in full screen mode. We will discuss the relevant numeric keypad and other keys here, and remind you of them as appropriate in later units.

Numeric Keypad Keys

These white keys are found on the right side of the keyboard. If you arc using dBASE II, or a personal computer other than an IBM or compatible, you may have to use the alternate versions which are listed below the keypad key name. Some of the less-often used key combinations are omitted.

　　　<ARROW KEYS> These keys move the cursor up, left, right, or down depending on the
　　　　　　　　　　specific application. <UP> and <DOWN> move a line or field at a time, while
　　　　　　　　　　<LEFT> and <RIGHT> move a character at a time.

Home　　　　　　　Moves the cursor one word to the left.
^A

End　　　　　　　　Moves the cursor one word to the right.
^F

^End　　　　　　　Exit and save from most editing situations.
^W

PgUp　　　　　　　Moves to the previous record or screen display.
^R

PgDn　　　　　　　Moves to the next record or screen display.
^C

Del ^G	Used to delete the character under the cursor.
Ins ^V	Used to toggle INSERT mode on or off. When it is ON, characters typed will be inserted and succeeding characters on the line will be pushed to the right. When it is OFF, a character typed will replace the character under the cursor.

Other Keys

<BACKSPACE> erases the character to the left of the cursor.

Esc ^Q	Exits without saving changes.
^N	Insert a new line or field definition.
^T	Erase one word to right of cursor.
^U	Mark a record for deletion, remove a field definition during Create or Modify Structure, remove a report field (column) during Modify Report.
^Y	Erase to end of field, or entire line.
Num Lock	Puts keypad in numeric mode. To use the <ARROW> keys, you must hold down the <SHIFT> key.
^Num Lock	The combination of Ctrl and Num Lock will pause the display -- use this to momentarily stop a list of data going by on the screen. Press the <SPACE> bar to resume the display.
Break	Break is the combination of Ctrl and Scroll Lock keys -- hold down Ctrl and press Scroll Lock. This will stop most printing and calculating processes.
PrtSc	The combination of <SHIFT>PrtSc will send a snapshot of the screen to the printer. Most of the figures in this book are modified screen prints. This capability is especially useful when you are having problems and no one is available to help you. Make a screen print and take that print to your instructor or friend.

STARTUP PROCEDURE

The exact procedure for starting dBASE III will vary from place to place, and perhaps from computer to computer.* Because of the size of the program, using dBASE III requires that

---

* If this is your first encounter with a personal computer, you should read Appendix A before proceeding.

you start the computer using two different disks. If you are using dBASE II, you probably do not need the a second diskette, both dBASE and the operating system will normally be on the same disk. You will need a configured copy of the appropriate program,* and a formatted disk to hold the files you will create.

Floppy Disk Systems

1. Put a formatted disk in drive B. This disk will hold the files that you create. Insert the disk with DOS in the Left (A) drive:

   a. For dBASE III, version 1.0, this is the special DOS disk created by your organization.

   b. For dBASE III, version 1.1, this is System Disk #1.

   c. For dBASE II, this is the only disk.

2. Reset or turn on the machine, as appropriate. Remember to enter the date and time as prompted.

3. The next step varies depending upon the specific program/version:

   a. For dBASE III, version 1.0, once the system is (re)loaded and the date and time set, remove the system disk and insert the dBASE III disk. The program is loaded and run by typing the command

      dbase<CR>

   b. For dBASE III, version 1.1, type the command

      dbase<CR>

      to load the program. At the appropriate time, you will be told to remove System Disk #1 and insert System Disk #2. The remainder of the program will be loaded.

   c. For dBASE II, type the command

      dbase<CR>

4. You should now see the Opening Screen. Figure 2-1 illustrates the dBASE III, version 1.0 Opening Screen. Figure 2-2 illustrates a dBASE II Opening Screen.

5. At the bottom of the screen, you will see a period. This is the command prompt. dBASE awaits your command. (dBASE II users, type SET DEFAULT TO B:)

---

* If your copy of dBASE III or dBASE II has not been configured, you or the person responsible for the software must perform the steps detailed in the "Installation" or "Setting Up" section of the manual which came with the software.

```
dBASE III  version 1.00  14 June 1984 IBM/MSDOS ***

COPYRIGHT (c) ASHTON-TATE 1984
AS AN UNPUBLISHED LICENSED PROPRIETARY WORK.
ALL RIGHTS RESERVED.

Use of this software and the other materials contained in the software
(the "Materials") has been provided under a Software License Agreement (please
read in full). In summary, Ashton-Tate grants you a paid-up, non-transferrable,
personal license to use the Materials only on a single or subsequent (but not
additional) computer terminal for fifty years from the time the sealed diskette
has been opened. You receive the right to use the Materials, but you do not
become the owner of them. You may not alter, decompile, or reverse-assemble the
software, and YOU MAY NOT COPY the Materials. The Materials are protected by
copyright, trade secrets, and trademark law, the violation of which can result
in civil damages and criminal prosecution.

dBASE, dBASE III and ASHTON-TATE are trademarks of Ashton-Tate.



Press the F1 key for help
Type a command (or ASSIST) and press the return key.

. _
```

FIGURE 2-1 The dBASE III Opening Screen
Copyright (C) Ashton-Tate, printed with permission.

```
A>dbase


Copyright (C) 1982 RSP Inc.

***  dBASE II/86  Ver 2.4      1 July 1983
. _
```

FIGURE 2-2 The dBASE II Opening Screen
Copyright (C) Ashton-Tate, printed with permission.

Hard Disk Systems

Most hard disk systems will have the dBASE programs installed on the hard disk. With dBASE III, version 1.0 you will have to use the System Disk in the disk drive so the program can verify that you are using a legitimate copy (this is not the case with dBASE II or version 1.1 of dBASE III).

1. Reset or turn on the machine, as appropriate. Remember to enter the date and time as prompted.

2. The next step varies depending upon the specific program/version:

    a. For dBASE III, version 1.0, once the system is (re)loaded and the date and time set, insert the dBASE III System Disk in the disk drive. The program is loaded and run by typing the command

        dbase<CR>

    b. For dBASE III, version 1.1, type the command

        dbase<CR>

    c. For dBASE II, type the command

        dbase<CR>

3. You should now see the Opening Screen. Figure 2-1 illustrates the dBASE III, version 1.0 Opening Screen. Figure 2-2 illustrates a dBASE II Opening Screen.

4. Put a formatted disk in the disk drive. This disk will hold the files that you create.

5. At the bottom of the screen, you will see a period. This is the command prompt. dBASE awaits your command. (dBASE II users, type SET DEFAULT TO A:)

REVIEW QUESTIONS

1. List the dBASE diskettes, and describe the uses of each.

2. How does dBASE use the following keyboard keys:

    *a. F1

    b. F2

    c. End

    d. Home

    *e. PgUp

*f. Del

*g. ^End

h. Esc

i. <BACKSPACE>

3. How do you load dBASE into the computer? Make note of any steps which differ in your organization from what is described above.

DOCUMENTATION RESEARCH

1a. Look at the dBASE III Reference Manual. What are the keywords and symbols used in command descriptions?

1b. Look at the dBASE II Reference Manual. What are the typographic conventions used in the manual?

2. Using the Index, determine which page has information about numeric accuracy.

3. Using the Index, determine which page discusses calculator operation.

4. Using the Index, determine which page contains the discussion of dBASE constraints.

5. Using the index to this book, answer questions 2., 3., and 4.

Unit

3

DATA FILE CREATION

It is time to move from discussion of data base concepts to use of data base concepts. In this unit, you will learn how to create a data file, how to enter data into the file, how to view the data in a file, how to edit entries in the file, and how to backup your data files. At the conclusion of this unit, your first activity on the computer will be to build a simple data file.

LEARNING OBJECTIVES

1. At the completion of this unit you should know

   a. the various types of fields,

   b. how to structure a data file.

2. At the completion of this unit you should be able to

   a. create a data file,

   b. enter data into the file,

   c. display the file contents,

   d. change entries in the file,

   e. backup your data files.

IMPORTANT COMMANDS

CREATE {filename}
USE {filename}
DISPLAY STRUCTURE
APPEND
DISPLAY
LIST
EDIT
QUIT

COMMANDING dBASE

dBASE commands consist of a command verb, usually followed by command parameters which may be nouns and conditional expressions. Only a portion of the many command variations are discussed in this manual, but those that are presented will serve in most situations and will provide a foundation for more sophisticated variations.

Commands may be issued at the dot prompt which you see once dBASE is loaded and ready for your input, and commands may also be included in command or program files, which will be discussed in Part Four. In either case, the command is entered by typing the command verb followed by any necessary parameters, and terminated by typing the <CR> key. Commands may be entered in upper or lower case. If you make a mistake entering a command, press the <BACKSPACE> key to back up and correct a character, or press the Esc key to start again.

Many command verbs and parameters may be abbreviated to the first four letters of the command, and may be capitalized or not. For instance, DISPLAY STATUS may be entered as DISP STAT, display status, or disp stat. In this manual, full length versions of commands will be used in most examples. When the example is contained within a paragraph, the command will be capitalized.

Braces -- { } -- are used to indicate where a command requires you to enter situation-specific information as a parameter. See, for instance, the CREATE command below, which requires you to enter a {filename} . In some instances, dBASE will prompt you for additional information if you fail to enter it with the command.

QUITTING

When using dBASE, it is very important to exit to the operating system before turning off the computer. Proper exit will insure that your work is saved. Failure to exit properly may result in the loss of some or all of the data in any open file.

The QUIT command will close (i.e., save) all open data files, terminate any programs in operation, and exit to the operating system (A>__ or C>__) prompt.

To give the command, type QUIT at the dot prompt. *Always use QUIT to exit dBASE.*

```
 B:datebook.dbf                              Bytes remaining:   4000
                                             Fields defined:       0


    field name  type      width  dec         field name  type      width  dec
    ================================         ================================
 1  _           Char/text





















 Names start with a letter; the remainder may be letters, digits, or underscore
```

FIGURE 3-1 Creating a Data File (I)

CREATING A DATA FILE

The CREATE command allows one to specify the field structure of a new file. The file will
have a .DBF extension added automatically by dBASE. The command is given from the dot
prompt, and you should specify the filename when you give the command. The general form
of the CREATE command is

    CREATE {filename}

{filename} can be any legal DOS filename of eight (8) or fewer characters from the set A-
Z, 0-9, and __ (underscore). Examples:

    create oklahoma
    create utah__dat

    Once the CREATE command is entered, the screen will clear and look like Figure 3-1.*
dBASE expects you to define each field in the file using four characteristics: Field
name, Type, Width, Decimal places. If you make a mistake. you can use the <ARROW> keys to

_____
* With dBASE II, you must enter the field characteristics in the format
name,type,width,decimals instead of filling in a form as illustrated for dBASE III.

```
 B:datebook.dbf                                  Bytes remaining:    3962
                                                 Fields defined:        4


      field name  type      width  dec          field name  type     width  dec
      ===============================           ===============================
  1   NAME        Char/text    15                
  2   AGE         Numeric       2     0          
  3   PHONE       Char/text    13                
  4   LAST_DATE   Date          8                
  5   _           Char/text                      




 Names start with a letter; the remainder may be letters, digits, or underscore
```

FIGURE 3-2 Creating a Data File (II)
Note: Items entered by the user are in **boldface**.

move around on the screen and correct the mistake before exiting the create process. If
you do not notice the mistake before you exit the create process, you will have to use the
MODIFY STRUCTURE command discussed in Unit 8.

Field Name

The field name begins with an alphabetic character, and may consist of up to 10 characters
from set of A-Z and 0-9. In dBASE III, the __ (underscore) character may also be used in
field names.* All letters will be converted to upper case. Each field name must be
unique within a database, but different databases may have fields with identical names.
To specify the field name in dBASE III, type the field name in the column below "field
name." If the name is less than 10 characters, press the <CR> key to move to the next
column, "type."

---

* In dBASE II the : (colon) character may be used in field names, but not the __
(underscore).

Field Type

The field type tells dBASE what type of data will be stored in the field. In dBASE III, type may be one of

    C   character string (anything printable)
    N   numeric (numbers, decimal point, leading - [minus] sign)
    L   logical (True or False, Yes or No)
    D   date* (in form 12/31/85)
    M   memo*

The choice of field type is confusing to novices. Use these guidelines:

If the field represents a yes/no or true/false data, then choose logical type.

If the field contains a date, then choose date type in dBASE III (and probably character type in dBASE II).

If the field contains numeric data that you will be performing calculations on or with, then choose numeric type.

If the field contains a large amount of text (over 50 characters), then choose memo type in dBASE III.

If none of the above apply, then choose character type.

Many fields that contain numbers should not be numeric type fields. If the number contains characters other than digits 0-9, . (period), or a leading - (minus sign), dBASE will not let you store it in a numeric field. Thus, social security numbers (e.g., 531-66-2876) and telephone numbers (e.g., 447-5996) must be character fields. Also, numbers with required leading zeros such as zip codes, (e.g., 02142) must be stored as character fields or the leading zero will be lost (i.e., 2142 instead of 02142). Finally, numbers which will be used as index keys should be stored as character type data.

dBASE III will assume that you want Char/text type. If that is your choice, press <CR> and the cursor will move to the "width" column. If you need a different type, press the key corresponding to that type. The cursor will move to the "width" column if you have specified numeric, or to the next field name if you have specified date, logic, or memo.

Field Width

For character and numeric types, the field width must be specified. This is the total width of the field -- character data may up to 254 bytes, numeric data is accurate to 15.9 digits.** Three field types have fixed width (logical data is of width 1, date data is

---

* In dBASE II, only character, numeric, and logical types are available. Dates and long text strings must be handled using one of these three types.
** 10 digits in dBASE II

```
Input data records now? (Y/N) No
. display structure
Structure for database : B:datebook.dbf
Number of data records :        0
Date of last update    : 06/14/85
Field  Field name  Type       Width    Dec
    1   NAME        Character     15
    2   AGE         Numeric        2
    3   PHONE       Character     13
    4   LAST_DATE   Date           8
** Total **                      39


.  _
```

FIGURE 3-3 Checking the Structure of a Data File
Note: Items entered by the user are in **boldface**.

width 8, and memo data is width 10) and dBASE III will not ask you to specify width for fields of those types.

Decimal Places

If the field type is numeric, you must specify the number of decimal places. Warning: the width must be greater than or equal to the number of decimal places *plus two* -- dBASE requires room for a leading zero and the decimal point. Decimal places are optional and not recommended for integer-only data.

See Figure 3-2 for an example of the data file creation process in dBASE III. The information will be the same. The following are legitimate field specifications:

NAME,C,15
AGE,N,2,0
PHONE,C,13   *allows format of (414)224-7534*
SALARY,N,9,2   *what's the maximum salary?*
EXEMPT,L,1

Pressing the <CR> key as the first character of a field name (in either version) terminates the create process. You will be asked if you wish to input data now? -- generally you should answer N (no), so you can check the structure before entering data.

Check

Before inputting data, it is wise to check the structure of the file you have created. Do so by typing the command DISPLAY STRUCTURE as illustrated in Figure 3-3. dBASE may respond with the message "No database file in use, enter filename." If so, enter the filename which you specified as part of the CREATE command.

Note that the structure displayed in Figure 3-3 is the same as the structure created in Figure 3-2. The total length of the structure is the sum of the field widths plus one -- the extra character is used to indicate "end of record" and whether or not the record is marked as "deleted" (cf. Unit 8). The DISPLAY STRUCTURE command may be given by typing the F5 key.

If you notice a mistake in the structure of the file, you will have to use the MODIFY STRUCTURE command discussed in Unit 8 to make corrections.

DATA ENTRY

Once the structure is verified, you may enter data into the file. All the data may be put in at one time, or data may be entered over several sessions. In either case, the process is the same: first the file is opened, then the data is entered.

Opening a File

The USE command is used to open a data file for subsequent dBASE operations. Before any operations can be performed on a previously created data file, the USE command must be given.   This command is given from the dot prompt, and you must specify the filename when you give the command. One form of the USE command is

    USE {filename}

Examples:

    use oklahoma
    use utah_dat

The USE command is also one method for saving your work because USE will close the previously open file before it opens a new one -- saving work to date to the disk. This happens even if the file you use next is the same as the file you were using. It is a good idea to [re-] USE {filename} every so often to make sure your work does not get lost. USE without a {filename} will close the file in use without opening another.

Adding Data to a File

The APPEND command will position you at the end of the data file and allow you to enter data into a new record (which then becomes the last record). The APPEND command may be given by typing the F9 key.

Once the APPEND command is issued, the screen will clear and you will be presented with a blank form (see Figure 3-4). Enter the information into the highlighted blocks on the form. If you try to enter non-numeric characters into numeric fields, dBASE will beep at you. If you enter an invalid date (such as 02/31/84) dBASE will print the message "Invalid Date" at the top of the screen and require you to reenter the date.

```
┌─────────────────────────────────────────────────────────────┐
│  Record No.        1                                         │
│  NAME            _                                           │
│  AGE                                                         │
│  PHONE                                                       │
│  LAST_DATE      /  /                                         │
│                                                              │
└─────────────────────────────────────────────────────────────┘
```

FIGURE 3-4 Entering Data (I)

If the item you are entering completely fills the field width, dBASE will beep and move to the next field. If the item does not fill the field, press <CR> to move to the next field. It is a good idea to watch the screen as you enter the first few records to see if you are getting what you want. See Figure 3-5 for an example of a completed record.

If you make a mistake, you may correct that mistake without leaving the append process. Use the <ARROW> keys to move around in the current record to the point of error, then use Del, Ins, and <BACKSPACE> as necessary to correct. If the mistake is on a previous record, use the PgUp key to move to that record. Once the mistake is corrected, PgDn key will take you to the point where you may continue appending.

Once the record is completed (i.e., the last field is filled in) you will be presented with a new blank record. You can append ad infinitum -- press <CR> at the first character of the first field of a new record to exit the append process.

Another command for adding data to a data file is the INSERT command, which allows you to insert a new record immediately after the current record (which may be first, last, or intermediate). INSERT BEFORE places the new record immediately before the current record. Only one record at a time is inserted. *I do not recommend using the INSERT command* because, under some circumstances, the last record in the data file is lost.

SAVING YOUR WORK

The USE command is one method for saving your work because USE will close (i.e., write all data to a disk file) the previously open file before it opens a new one. This happens even if the file you use next is the same as the file you were using when you gave the command. It is a good idea to [re-] USE {filename} every so often to make sure your work does not get lost. USE without a {filename} will close the file in use without opening another.

The QUIT command also saves your work by closing all open files before exiting to the operating system.

```
  ┌─────────────────────────────────────────────────────────────────┐
  │                                                                   │
  │  Record No.        4                                              │
  │  NAME           Grouch, Oscar                                     │
  │  AGE            21                                                │
  │  PHONE          (801)581-1234                                     │
  │  LAST_DATE      11/27/84                                          │
  │                                                                   │
  │                                                                   │
  └─────────────────────────────────────────────────────────────────┘
```

FIGURE 3-5 Entering Data (II)
Note: Items entered by the user are in **boldface**.

VIEWING THE DATA IN A DATA FILE

There are two commands used for viewing data from the dot prompt. You will find use for both during your dBASE experience.

Viewing a Limited Set of Records

The DISPLAY command shows all or part of the data file in use:

DISPLAY   *shows the current record*
DISPLAY NEXT 10   *will show the current record and the nine succeeding records*
DISPLAY ALL   *shows all records, one screenful at a time*

You may also display only those records which meet some specified criterion. This version of the command is

DISPLAY FOR {condition}

which will show only those records for which {condition} is true. For example, DISPLAY FOR (SALARY > 30000) would show only those records in which the salary field had a value greater than 30000. I recommend that you enclose the {condition} in parentheses so dBASE knows exactly what you are specifying.   Conditions are the topic of Unit 4.

When you are interested in a few specific fields, you may use the following

DISPLAY {list}

to display only those fields listed, e.g., DISPLAY NAME,SALARY .

In dBASE III, the DISPLAY command may be given by typing the F8 key.*

---

* In dBASE II, the DISPLAY command is given by typing the F2 key.

```
. list
Record#   NAME              AGE PHONE        LAST_DATE
       1  Cary, Bill         25 (503)447-1520 12/12/84
       2  Smith, John        33 (414)224-7533 12/25/82
       3  French, Willa      21 (212)765-5996 01/14/80
       4  Grouch, Oscar      21 (801)581-1234 11/27/84

. _
```

FIGURE 3-6 Listing Data
Note: Item entered by the user is in **boldface**.

Viewing All Records

The LIST command is similar to DISPLAY, except that LIST will display all records, without waiting after each screenful. Very handy command for a quick glance at your data file. The LIST command is illustrated in Figure 3-6. The LIST command may be given by typing the F3 key.

LIST may also be constrained by a logical condition, like the DISPLAY FOR {condition} example above, and display only certain fields, like the DISPLAY {list} example.

To make a printed copy of your data file, issue the dBASE III command LIST TO PRINT . A logical {condition} may be included as in LIST FOR (SALARY > 30000) TO PRINT .*

EDITING DATA

One of the main reasons for listing data is for proofreading. To correct errors, use the EDIT command which allows you to selectively change the data in a data file field. Initiate editing by either EDIT (in which case you will edit the current record) or EDIT {record number} to edit any other specific record. In either case, you may then selectively change data. (Figure 3-7)

Use the <ARROW> keys to move around in the record to the point of error, then use Del, Ins, and <BACKSPACE> as necessary to correct. If there is an error on other record, use the PgUp or PgDn key to move to that record. Once all mistakes are corrected, type ^End (Ctrl-End) to terminate process and save changes, or press the PgDn or PgUp keys to move to the next or previous record in the file, which you may then edit. To terminate editing, press ^End.

---

* To make a printed copy of your data file using dBASE II, type the following sequence of commands from the dot prompt:

    set print on
    list
    set print off

```
Record No.      2
NAME        Smithe, Jon
AGE         33
PHONE       (414)224-7533
LAST_DATE   12/25/82
```

FIGURE 3-7 Editing Data

To abort editing, press the Esc key.

For instance, to change John Smith to Jon Smithe, type EDIT 2, which will put you at the beginning of the NAME field in the second record. <RIGHT ARROW> to the , in the name, press the Ins key, then press the e , which will be inserted before the , . Next <RIGHT ARROW> to the h and press the Del key which will delete the h and move the n to the left. Press Ctrl-End to terminate editing.

The EDIT command may be given by typing the F10 key.

BACKUP

"Backup" is one of those computer words that is a noun, an adjective, and a verb. A backup is a copy of the original file, usually stored in a safe place in case something happens to the original to render it unusable. Backup disks contain backups. To backup is to make backup copies.

There are a multitude of gremlins lurking out there that will ruin your day if you are not prepared. You may inadvertently ruin a file by making the wrong changes and saving it. Disks occasionally develop bad spots which make previously saved files unreadable. Spills (coffee, soda) and ashes may ruin a disk. Someone may steal your briefcase (backpack) or you may misplace your box of disks. Unexpected electromagnetic radiation may erase disks. (Telephones, magnetic paper clip holders, and library security systems all look innocent -- but any of these may damage your disks). Disks left in cars may be damaged by extreme heat or cold.

You should become obsessive about making backup copies of your work. I recommend that you make a backup every time you finish a session at the computer. There are several levels of backup:

same disk, different filename

different disk, same location

different disk, different location

Same Disk, Different Filename

This method saves the file under two different names. If something goes wrong with one version of the file, the other may be OK.

To implement, use the COPY command (discussed in more detail in Unit 7) to copy the file to another database with a different name, e.g., COPY TO RAW2 .

This provides a minimal level of protection. It does protect you from random failures which affect single data files, and may provide you a previous version if you make unwanted changes. It will not help, however, if something (like a spilled cup of coffee) destroys the entire disk.

Different Disk, Same Location

This method saves the file on two different disks, under the same filename. If one disk gets destroyed, the other is available.

To implement, QUIT from the dBASE. When you have the PC-DOS command prompt (A>_), put the backup disk in drive A:, leaving your data disk in drive B:.* (The backup disk must have been formatted previously, and may contain other files.) Type the command

    copy b:*.*<CR>

which will copy all files from the B: disk to the A: disk. Be careful: if you type the command incorrectly, or put the disks in the wrong drives, you may copy old versions of files over new versions. I recommend putting a tab over the write-protect notch of the original disk to prevent wrong-way copying.

This provides additional protection. Keep the backup disk in the box except when you are using it, so that most local disasters (such as the spilled coffee) will not affect it. You are still at risk, however, for disasters such as theft of your backpack, fire, or electromagnetic fields.

Different Disk, Different Location

This method saves the file on two different disks, under the same filename. The disks are stored in separate locations, so that if the disk box gets destroyed, the backup is available.

This is implemented in the same manner as version 2, except that you have to find a place to store the backup. If you have a desk or locker at work/school, you could leave a copy there and take the other copy home. You might ask a friend to take your backup disk. Some computer areas have a place to store disks, and you could leave the backup there.

_____

* If you are using a hard disk system, ask your instructor for the most efficient manner to create different-disk backups. The commands listed will usually work, but your organization may have software which provides a better way.

This provides the greatest protection. It is very unlikely that the same disaster would destroy both of your disks.

GUIDED ACTIVITY

This activity requires you to use the data file creation commands. It includes two **CHECKPOINT** questions, the answers to which are found in Appendix B.

1. Follow the startup procedure for your version of dBASE as outlined in Unit 2.

2. We want to create a file which will replace our personal address book, the one in which we keep the names and numbers of our friends. The first step in the process is to look at a list of the data to determine file structure. Such a list appears in Table 3-1.

3. We will name the file DATEBOOK. Looking at the data, we decide to name the fields NAME, AGE, PHONE, and LAST_DATE.* (Why the _ [underscore] in LAST_DATE?) For type, we choose character for NAME and PHONE, numeric for AGE, and for LAST_DATE we choose date (dBASE III) or character (dBASE II). Widths are 15, 2, 13, and 8, respectively.

4. Give the command CREATE DATEBOOK . The screen will look like Figure 3-1. Enter the structure information, until the screen looks like Figure 3-2. When dBASE asks for the description of the fifth field, press <CR> to exit the create process. Answer n to the "Input data records now?" question.

5. Give the command DISPLAY STRUCTURE (or press the F5 key). The structure should look like Figure 3-3. If the structure is different, ask your instructor what to do, or read "Modifying the Structure of a Data File" in Part Two.

6. If the structure is acceptable, the next step is to enter the data. Type the command USE DATEBOOK to insure that the file is open, then APPEND (or the F9 key). The screen will now look like Figure 3-4. Enter the data from Table 3-1 into each record. (You may wish to review the section "Adding data to a file" before you start entering data.) As you are entering data, the screen will look like Figure 3-5.

7. After entering Oscar Grouch's data, you will be presented with a blank form for Record No. 5. Press <CR> before typing anything, and dBASE will terminate the append process.

8. To proofread, type the command LIST (or F3). Check what you see on the screen against Table 3-1 or Figure 3-6. If there are differences, make a note so they can be corrected in the next step.

9. To complicate things, John Smith joined a rock group and changed his name to Jon Smithe. Using the command EDIT 2 and the example in the section "Editing Data" above, make the change. Also correct any errors in other entries. Remember to type Ctrl-End to exit editing.

---

* In dBASE II, the field should be named LAST:DATE, and character type.

TABLE 3-1 List of Friends

NAME	AGE	PHONE	LAST DATE
Cary, Bill	25	(503)447-1520	12/12/84
Smith, John	33	(414)224-7533	12/25/82
French, Willa	21	(212)765-5996	01/14/80
Grouch, Oscar	21	(801)581-1234	11/27/84

10. List the data again to check the results of your editing. If the file is correct,
    and if a printer is available, type the command LIST TO PRINT to obtain a printed
    (a.k.a. hardcopy) listing of your file.

11. When you have completed all of the above, give the command QUIT to exit dBASE.
    From the DOS (A>_) prompt, give the command DIR B: (or DIR A: if you are using
    a hard disk PC) to make sure that you have a file named DATEBOOK.DBF on your disk.

12. Make a "different disk" backup copy of your work.

✔ CHECKPOINT
  What must you do before you make a different disk backup copy?

_____

✔ CHECKPOINT
  What command will you give to make a different disk backup copy?

_____

13. If everything is proper, turn off the computer and return the dBASE software to the
    Lab Supervisor.

REVIEW QUESTIONS

1. List the types of fields in dBASE III (or II), state the maximum or default width,
   and indicate a use for each.

2. What field name, type, width, and decimals would be most appropriate for each of the
   following:

   *a. stock market ticker symbols, e.g., IBM, APPL, T, DEC, X

   *b. stock prices, e.g., 8.125, 108.0, 16.35

   *c. telephone numbers, e.g., (414)224-1440, (212)667-7329

   d. social security numbers, e.g., 543-55-2786

*e. smoker or non-smoker category

*f. dates, e.g., 1/1/86, 7/4/76

g. zip codes, e.g., 06981, 97701, 53234

h. zip+4 codes, e.g., 06981-2258, 97701-1143, 53234-5011

3. Look at Table 1-1. What structure would you create for the data in that table? Specify field name, type, width, and decimals for each field needed.

4. Why should you backup your data?

5. Develop a backup system that will work for you. Consider most likely hazards to your data, organization policies about using data, and access to computers. Describe the system.

DOCUMENTATION RESEARCH

Using the reference manual, determine the answer to the following questions which deal with the commands discussed in this Unit. I recommend you also write the page number by the discussion of the command, above.

1. CREATE -- how can you delete a field during the creation process?

2. USE -- if a file extension is not specified (the usual case), what extension is assumed by dBASE?

3. APPEND -- how do you enter data into a memo field?

4. DISPLAY -- what type of field is not normally displayed?

5. LIST -- what is the major difference between this command and DISPLAY?

6. EDIT -- how do you abort editing?

7. QUIT -- what may happen if you reset the computer without using this command?

8. Look up the section of the manual entitled "Error Recovery" (dBASE II) or "Running dBASE III" and determine what to do if you make a typing error when entering a command.

Application

A CHEZ JACQUES (I)

In this exercise, you will create one file and edit two others which will be used in subsequent exercises.

1. Start by signing out the dBASE manual and software, as well as the EXERCISES disk.

2. Insert the EXERCISES disk in the Left (A) drive. Insert a formatted disk in the B drive.* This disk will hold the files that you create and edit.

3. Reset or turn on the machine, as appropriate. Remember to enter the date and time as prompted.

4. Once the system is loaded and the date and time set you should see the DOS command prompt (A>_). Give the commands

        copy fin_good.dbf b:<CR>
        copy mix.dbf b:<CR>

    which will copy two database files from the EXERCISES disk to your disk.

5. Once the copying is finished, remove the EXERCISES disk and insert the dBASE III disk. Follow the startup procedure for your version of dBASE as outlined in Unit 2.

6. You have been hired by Jacques LaFayette to establish a DBMS for the Chez Jacques Hamburger Château. The first step is to create files which contain a list of the raw materials, the menu, and the mix of ingredients in the menu items. You decide to create the raw materials file yourself, and to hire someone else to create the other two files.

---

* If you are using a fixed disk PC, your instructor will give you instructions for accomplishing steps 2-4.

7. To begin the process, you must determine the structure for the raw materials file, which you will name RAW_MATL. Look at Table 1-1. Note that there are five columns of information, therefore five fields will be needed. Appropriate field names would be RMID (raw materials identification), DESC (description), COST (unit cost), INVENTORY (quantity on hand), and LAST_ORDER (date of last order).

   To complete the determination of the structure, consider each field in turn. For RMID, the type should be Character because leading zeros are important and no arithmetic is to be performed. (As we will see later, this field will also be an index key.) The minimum necessary field width is 4 bytes.

   For DESC, the type must be Character. What is the minimum field width?

   For COST, the type should be Numeric because we anticipate that we will be doing mathematics on this field. How many decimal places are needed, and what is the minimum field width?

   For INVENTORY, the type should be Numeric because we anticipate that we will be doing mathematics on this field. How many decimal places are needed, and what is the minimum field width?

   For LAST_ORDER, the type should be Date (in dBASE III) because this field contains date data.* The field width defaults to 8 bytes in dBASE III.

   Therefore, the structure should be

Field	Field name	Type	Width	Dec
1	RMID	Character	4	
2	DESC	Character	15	
3	COST	Numeric	8	2
4	INVENTORY	Numeric	3	
5	LAST_ORDER	Date	8	

8. Give the command CREATE RAW_MATL and create the file as defined above.

9. Once the file is created, give the commands USE RAW_MATL and DISPLAY STRUCTURE to determine whether or not you have defined all fields correctly. If there are errors, consult with your instructor or refer to the section "Modifying the Structure of a Data File" in Part Two.

10. If the structure is acceptable, give the APPEND command and input the data from Table 1-1. Type the data exactly as it appears, including punctuation and capitalization, because any differences may frustrate you as you do later activities and exercises.

---

* In dBASE II, the date type is not available, so we must use Character type. The field width should be set at 8 bytes.

TABLE A-1 Data in the Finished Goods File

Record#	FGID	DESC	SELL_PRICE	INVENTORY
1	1016	Apple Pie	0.79	0
2	1001	Big Jac	1.35	0
3	1007	Cheese Burger	0.69	0
4	1017	Cherry Pie	0.79	0
5	1010	Giant Coke	0.99	0
6	1013	Giant Sprite	0.99	0
7	1006	Hamburger	0.59	0
8	1011	Large Coke	0.79	0
9	1008	Large Fries	0.67	0
10	1014	Large Sprite	0.79	0
11	1002	Jac Meal /Co/Ap	2.25	0
12	1003	Jac Meal /Co/Ch	2.25	0
13	1004	Jac Meal /Sp/Ap	2.25	0
14	1005	Jac Meal /Sp/Ch	2.25	0
15	1012	Regular Coke	0.49	0
16	1009	Regular Fries	0.43	0
17	1015	Regular Sprite	0.49	0

11. When data for all 19 records has been input, exit the append process by typing <CR> when presented with the form for Record No. 20. Type the command LIST to see the data on the screen. Make a note of any discrepancies. The field names will be different in your list from those in Table 1-1.

12. If there are discrepancies, give the command EDIT #, where # is the record number with the error, and correct the data.

13. When you are happy with RAW_MATL, you must check the FIN_GOOD and MIX files against Tables A-1 and A-2. You will note that the person who entered the FIN_GOOD data apparently got the restaurants mixed up. The procedure for each is the same:

use fin_good	*open the file*
display all *or*	*list on screen*
list to print	*or printer*
	proofread
edit #	*correct records with errors*
	(# is the number of a record with an error)

14. When all files are perfect, type the command QUIT to exit dBASE. From the DOS (A>__) prompt, give the command DIR B: to make sure that you have files named RAW_MATL.DBF, MIX.DBF, and FIN_GOOD.DBF on your disk. Remember to backup your work. If everything is proper, turn off the computer and return the dBASE software and the EXERCISES disk to the Lab Supervisor.

TABLE A-2 Data in the Mix File

Record#	FGID	RMID	RM_QTY	Record#	FGID	RMID	RM_QTY
1	1001	0001	2	42	1004	0018	1
2	1001	0002	2	43	1004	0016	1
3	1001	0003	1	44	1005	0001	2
4	1001	0004	2	45	1005	0002	2
5	1001	0005	4	46	1005	0003	1
6	1001	0006	1	47	1005	0004	2
7	1001	0007	1	48	1005	0005	4
8	1002	0001	2	49	1005	0006	1
9	1002	0002	2	50	1005	0007	1
10	1002	0003	1	51	1005	0012	11
11	1002	0004	2	52	1005	0014	1
12	1002	0005	4	53	1005	0010	4
13	1002	0006	1	54	1005	0018	1
14	1002	0007	1	55	1005	0017	1
15	1002	0011	11	56	1006	0001	1
16	1002	0014	1	57	1006	0005	2
17	1002	0010	4	58	1006	0008	1
18	1002	0018	1	59	1006	0009	1
19	1002	0016	1	60	1007	0001	1
20	1003	0001	2	61	1007	0005	2
21	1003	0002	2	62	1007	0008	1
22	1003	0003	1	63	1007	0009	1
23	1003	0004	2	64	1007	0004	1
24	1003	0005	4	65	1008	0010	6
25	1003	0006	1	66	1008	0019	1
26	1003	0007	1	67	1009	0010	4
27	1003	0011	11	68	1009	0018	1
28	1003	0014	1	69	1010	0011	15
29	1003	0010	4	70	1010	0015	1
30	1003	0018	1	71	1011	0011	11
31	1003	0017	1	72	1011	0014	1
32	1004	0001	2	73	1012	0011	7
33	1004	0002	2	74	1012	0013	1
34	1004	0003	1	75	1013	0012	15
35	1004	0004	2	76	1013	0015	1
36	1004	0005	4	77	1014	0012	11
37	1004	0006	1	78	1014	0014	1
38	1004	0007	1	79	1015	0012	7
39	1004	0012	11	80	1015	0013	1
40	1004	0014	1	81	1016	0016	1
41	1004	0010	4	82	1017	0017	1

[continued in right column]

Part

2

INTERMEDIATE DATA BASE OPERATIONS

In this part, we begin to use the computer to accomplish data base inquiry operations. Because most inquiry operations require selection or computation, the first unit in this part deals with the operators and functions available in dBASE. Summary statistics are covered in the second unit.

The third unit in this part discusses methods for ordering data in a file and for locating specific records, followed by units dealing with system interface and data file modification.

We will also learn several ways to extract data from our data files and output that data in the format we desire. Possible output formats include Reports, Labels, and Lists. You may also send data to other applications programs which will format it as necessary.

The exercises in this part will provide practice in using the operations discussed.

Unit

4 CONDITIONS AND EXPRESSIONS

dBASE allows you to perform simple mathematic operations as well as complex search routines. This unit provides the basis for those procedures: operators which join components of an expression and functions which modify the meaning of an expression.

Do not try to memorize this material. Skim the unit to see how the material is arranged and work the review problems at the end of the unit. You will need to refer to this unit often, but you do not need to memorize everything which follows.

LEARNING OBJECTIVES

1. At the completion of this unit you should know

   a. the difference between logical conditions and computed expressions,

   b. what "order of precedence" means,

   c. how each of the operators is used in expressions and conditions,

   d. what the various categories of functions are.

2. At the completion of this unit you should be able to

   a. write expressions and conditions using the various operators,

   b. write expressions and conditions using functions.

IMPORTANT COMMANDS

?
LIST

LOGICAL CONDITIONS VS. COMPUTED EXPRESSIONS

We will make use of two general types of expressions. The one type will be called **logical conditions**, the other will be called **computed expressions**. Logical conditions are used with dBASE commands to limit the scope of a command, e.g., LIST *FOR SALARY>10000* . The italicized portion of that command is a logical condition. Logical conditions are usually preceded by the preposition FOR and consist of one or more logical and comparison operators and logical-type data, usually combined with computed expressions, functions and character, date, or numeric data.

Computed expressions are used as index keys, in lists and reports, for computation of values, and as part of a logical condition, e.g., LIST FOR *COST*INVENTORY>10* , where the italicized portion is the computed expression. Computed expressions consist of functions, arithmetic and string operators, and character, date, and numeric data.

One of the most common difficulties experienced by beginning dBASE users is the confusion of logical conditions and computed expressions. *Remember: If you wish to limit the scope of an operation, use a* logical condition. *If you wish to obtain a result, use a* computed expression.

THE CALCULATOR

dBASE provides a very handy command which is called the "calculator" or "what is" command. The command itself is simple:

? {expression list}

{expression list} may be any computed expression consisting of mathematical formulas, field names, memory variables, or a combination. In its simplest form, this command may be used as a calculator: ? 65-18 will display 47.00 on the screen. When field names are included in the {expression list}, the contents of the fields in the current record will be used: ? NAME will display the contents of the name field of the current record (the concept of current record is discussed in Unit 6). A command such as ? SALARY*1.25 will tell you what the salary would be after a 25% raise. The current contents of the field (name, salary) is not changed.

OPERATORS

Operators are the glue that binds elements of expressions together. Most of us are familiar with operators such as the + sign:

2 + 2

In dBASE, the elements of expressions may be data file field names, memory variables (discussed in Part Three), or values contained within the expression itself.

Order of Precedence

Order of precedence refers to the priority of calculation. Expressions are evaluated from left to right, with sub-expressions enclosed by parentheses ( ) evaluated first, and those operators higher in the list evaluated before operators lower in the list.

For instance, from algebra we remember that

$$\frac{6^2}{12} = \frac{36}{12} = 3$$

and not

$$\frac{6^2}{12} = \frac{1}{2}^2 = \frac{1}{4}$$

The same situation will occur in dBASE, where

$6\text{^}2/12 = 3$

Arithmetic Operators

Arithmetic can be performed on numeric and date fields or variables, and values in expressions.

Arithmetic operators in order of precedence:

unary +,-	the sign (positive or negative) of a numeric expression
**,^	exponentiation*
*,/	multiplication and division
binary +,-	addition and subtraction

Using Arithmetic Operators in Expressions. Arithmetic operators are used to perform operations on the contents of fields (represented by field names), memory variables, values, and functions within expressions. In the following examples, assume that fields named FIELD1, FIELD2, ... FIELD6 all contain numeric values:

? field1+field2	*field FIELD1 is added to field FIELD2 and the sum is displayed on the screen*
? field1*field3	*displays the product of fields FIELD1 and FIELD3*
? field1^field4	*FIELD1 to the FIELD4[th] power**

---

* Exponentiation is not available in dBASE II.

? (field1+field2+field3)/field5	*computes and displays the sum of fields FIELD1, FIELD2 and FIELD3 divided by FIELD5*
? field4/field5+field6	*FIELD6 plus FIELD4 divided by FIELD5*
? field4/(field5+field6)	*FIELD4 divided by sum of FIELD5 and FIELD6*

String Operators

A string is a character field, a character variable, or a string of characters enclosed by
'...', "...", or [...] symbols.

The string operators have equal precedence, and are therefore evaluated left to
right:

$ *substring comparison*, if A and B are character fields, A$B will be true if
and only if string A is equal to B, or is contained in B . This operator
is used in logical conditions.

+   *concatenation*, connects the strings end to end. Blanks in either
string are retained. This operator is used in computed expressions.

Using String Operators in Expressions. String operators are used to tie together fields
(represented by field names), memory variables, strings, and functions into expressions.
In the following examples, assume that fields named FIELD7, FIELD8, and FIELD9 all
contain character data:

FIELD7 = 'ABCDEF'
FIELD8 = "GHIJKL"
FIELD9 = [DEFGHI]

? field7+field8	*displays ABCDEFGHIJKL*
? field9$field7	*will display .F. (false) because 'DEFGHI' is not in 'ABCDEF'*
? field9$(field7+field8)	*will display .T. (true)*
? field9$(field8+field7)	*.F. (false) because characters not in same order*

Comparison Operators

Comparisons can be performed between character, numeric and date fields or variables, and
strings/values in conditions. Both items being compared must be of the same type. These
operators generate logical results (true or false) which are used primarily in data file
search routines.

All comparison operators have equal precedence, and are therefore evaluated left to right:

<	less than
>	greater than
=	equal to
<>	not equal to (dBASE III only)
#	not equal to
<=	less than or equal to
>=	greater than or equal to
$	substring comparison (see above)

Logical Operators

Logical operators are used to tie two logical conditions together. These operators generate logical results (true or false) which are used primarily in data file search routines.

Logical operators in order of precedence:

.NOT.   changes true to false and false to true

.AND.   both conditions must be true for the total to be true

.OR.   if either condition is true, then the total is true

Using Comparison and Logical Operators. You may recall the DISPLAY FOR {condition} command discussed in Unit 3. Comparison and logical operators are used to build the {condition}.

Below are example commands using logical conditions. Each of the commands will list or display all records for which the logical condition is true.

list for (field1 = field2)
display for (field1 <= field3)
list for .not. (field3 >= field5) to print
display field2, field3 for ((field7 $ field8) .or. .not. (field3 > field1))
list field8 for (field4 < 10000) to print

When the *field type* is logical, then the logical {condition} may simply consist of the name of the field. For instance, if we have a field named SMOKER which is True if the person smokes and False otherwise, then

list for .not.smoker

will provide a list of all who do not smoke.

The comparison operators may also be used to compare character type data. One character string may less than or greater than another string based on the character order. (Character order is displayed in Table 6-1.) Also, two strings may be tested for equality. The strings are equal if they are exactly the same, or if the right-hand character string is identical to the starting characters of the left-hand character string:

? 'Rosenbaum' = 'Rose'   *yields .T. because the string on the right matches the beginning characters of the string on the left*

? 'Rose' = 'Rosenbaum'   *yields .F. because the string on the right is longer*

FUNCTIONS

Functions are used to form all or part of an expression. What follows is a partial list. See the appropriate reference manual if you need a complete list and more detailed explanations. dBASE III provides more functions, and some function names were changed from dBASE II. Differences are noted in the lists which follow.

The terms in parentheses which follow a function are called arguments of the function. Some functions require empty arguments, i.e., ( ) which enclose nothing. For the other functions, the argument must be a specific type, either character string, numeric, or date.

Character String Functions

Functions in this group deal with character and text strings.

    &   *macro function*, substitutes the contents of a character-type memory variable into an expression. Used primarily in command files (Part Three of this manual).

AT(char string 1,char string 2) *substring search function*, yields an integer whose value is the character number in char string 2 which begins a substring identical to char string 1.*

       ? at('ross','across')   *yields the result 3*

CHR(numeric expression) *number to character function*, yields the ASCII character equivalent of the numeric expression. Usually used to send a control code to a printer.

LEN(char string) *length function*, this function yields an integer whose value is the number of characters in the named string.

       ? len('Mike')   *yields the result 4*

---

* In dBASE II, the function is @(char string 1,char string 2).

LOWER(char string) *lower case function*, yields the same string as the char string except all letters are converted to lower case.*

> ? lower('Ross')   *yields ross*

STR(numeric expression,length,decimals) *string function*, evaluates a numeric expression and yields a character string, decimals specifier is optional.

> ? str(95.6,6,2)   *yields   95.60*

SUBSTR(char expression,start,length) *substring function*, forms a character string from the specified part of another string.**

> ? substr('across',2,5)   *will yield cross*

TRIM(char string) *trim function*, removes trailing blanks from a character string. Usually used when the contents of a field is shorter than the length of the field.

UPPER(char string) *upper case function*, yields the same string as the char string except that all letters are converted to upper case.***

> ? upper('Ross')   *yields ROSS*

Numeric Functions

dBASE III contains a few numeric functions which are not available in dBASE II. If exponents, logarithms, and square roots are important, then you may not be able to do your work in dBASE II.

EXP(numeric expression) *exponential function*, returns the value of e^x.*

INT(numeric expression) *the integer function*, evaluates the numeric expression and discards the fractional part to yield an integer value. Truncates, does not round.

> ? int(6.75)   *yields 6*

LOG(numeric expression) *log function*, returns the natural logarithm [$\log_e$] of a given number.*

ROUND(numeric expression,decimal) *rounding function*, rounds the numeric expression to specified number of decimal places. *ROUND does not always work correctly with negative numbers*.*

SQRT(numeric expression) *square root function*, returns the square root of a positive number.*

---

* Not available in dBASE II.
** In dBASE II, the function is $(char expression,start,length).
*** In dBASE II, the function is !(char string).

VAL(char string) *string to numeric function*, forms an integer from a character string made up of digits, signs, and up to one decimal point.

? val('236.50abc09')   *yields 236.50*

Date and Time Functions

dBASE II has only one date and time function: DATE( ). dBASE III has expanded the list to 10 functions, some of which are discussed below.

DATE( ) *date function*, returns the system date in the form MM/DD/YY. If you set the date properly when loading the system, this will be today's date.

if the system date is 01/01/85, then
? date( )   *yields 01/01/85*

CDOW(date variable) *character day of week function*, returns the name of the day of the week from a date variable.*

if the system date is 01/01/85, then
? cdow(date( ))   *yields Tuesday*

CMONTH(date variable) *character month function*, returns the name of the month from a date variable.*

if the system date is 01/01/85, then
? cmonth(date( ))   *yields January*

CTOD(char expression) *character to date function*, creates a date variable from a character string. Used as precursor to date arithmetic.*

if the system date is 11/09/85 and I want to know how long it is to New Year's Day 1986, I would use the following:
? ctod('01/01/86')-date( )

DTOC(date expression) *date to character function*, creates a character string from a date variable. Used to create a text string for headings, etc.*

TIME( ) *time function*, returns the system time in the form hh:mm:ss. If you set the time properly when loading the system, this will be the current time.*

File and Record Functions

Functions in this group are primarily used in command (program) files, and will be discussed in Part Three of this manual.

---

* Not available in dBASE II.

Functions not Discussed

Function	Availability dBASE III	dBASE II
ASC(char string)	yes	no
COL( )	yes	no
DAY(date variable)	yes	no
DOW(date variable)	yes	no
MONTH(date variable)	yes	no
PCOL( )	yes	no
PROW( )	yes	no
RANK(char string)	no	yes
ROW( )	yes	no
SPACE(number)	yes	no
TYPE(expression)	yes	yes
YEAR(date variable)	yes	no

CONSTRAINED LISTS

There are many methods for extracting data from dBASE files and presenting that data in a report format. The quickest method is to use the LIST command to produce a list of the data. The normal list output includes all records, field names, and record numbers. In this section, we discuss how to eliminate some aspects of lists which you may consider extraneous.

Look at Figure 4-1. At the top, you will notice that the RAW_MATL file has been opened with its index. Then the command LIST FOR COST>.10 was given which produced a standard list, with record numbers and field names, but limited to those items which cost more than 10 cents.

In many cases, the record numbers will be unnecessary. The second listing was created with the command LIST OFF FOR COST>.10 . The OFF keyword works with both LIST and DISPLAY commands to suppress record number information.

In dBASE III, standard list format includes field names. To suppress field names on lists and displays, give the command SET HEADING OFF which will remain in effect until you exit dBASE, or give the command SET HEADING ON .*

If field names are specified with the command, then only those fields will be listed. For instance, the command LIST DESC,COST would list only those fields for all records (since there is no FOR {condition}).

Lists may also contain computed expressions. To list all raw materials, with present costs and costs+15%, the command LIST OFF DESC,COST,(1.15*COST) would be given.

The listing may be sent to the printer by adding the phrase TO PRINT to any of the above.

---

* Field names are never included in dBASE II lists, so this command is not available in dBASE II.

```
. use raw_matl index raw_matl
. list for cost>.10
Record#    RMID DESC                    COST INVENTORY LAST_ORDER
      18   0007 sesame seed bun         0.12       400 10/08/85
       9   0016 apple pie               0.16       346 08/15/85
      13   0017 cherry pie              0.14       200 09/19/85
   .
. list off for cost>.10
 RMID DESC                    COST INVENTORY LAST_ORDER
 0007 sesame seed bun         0.12       400 10/08/85
 0016 apple pie               0.16       346 08/15/85
 0017 cherry pie              0.14       200 09/19/85
   .
. set heading off
. list off for cost>.10
 0007 sesame seed bun         0.12 400 10/08/85
 0016 apple pie               0.16 346 08/15/85
 0017 cherry pie              0.14 200 09/19/85
   .
   . _
```

FIGURE 4-1 Variations of the LIST Command
Note: Items entered by the user are in **boldface**

GUIDED ACTIVITY

This activity requires you to conduct simple inquiry operations using the operators and functions discussed in this unit.

1. Follow the startup procedure for your version of dBASE as outlined in Unit 2.

2. USE RAW_MATL, which you created in Application A. (If your instructor did not assign Application A, a copy of RAW_MATL will be provided.)

3. List, on the printer, all materials for which the cost is less than 0.10.

    This requires that you know a few things. First, how to direct a list to the printer (Unit 3). Second, how to write an condition which is true only when the cost is less than 0.10. Finally, how to use the condition with the LIST command. Your screen will look similar to the top of Figure 4-1 after you have executed this command.

✔**CHECKPOINT**
What command do you use to accomplish this list?

4. Inventory value is defined as the product of the cost per unit and the inventory quantity. List, on the printer, all materials for which the inventory value is greater than 10.00 .

✔ **CHECKPOINT**
What command do you use to prepare this list?

_____

5. List, on the printer, all materials which are inventoried by the ounce (oz.). You will have to use the substring comparison operator.

✔ **CHECKPOINT**
What command do you use to develop this list?

_____

6. Print a list of all raw material items in which Chez Jacques has more than $50.00 invested. The list should not include record numbers or field names.

✔ **CHECKPOINT**
What commands do you use to print this list?

_____

7. When you have completed all of the above, give the command QUIT to exit dBASE. Turn off the computer and return the dBASE software to the Lab Supervisor.

REVIEW QUESTIONS

1. What is the difference between logical conditions and computed expressions?

*2. What does "order of precedence" mean?

3. What are the various categories of functions?

4. Assume that the following fields have the values indicated. Determine whether the conditions are true or false.

Field	Type	Value
NAME	C	Fred
COLOR	C	RED
AGE	N	25
SIZE	N	46

*a. (name $ color)

*b. (color $ name)

*c. (color $ upper(name))

   *d. (age < size)

    e. (age # size)

   *f. .not. (age > size)

   *g. (color $ name) .and. (age < size)

   *h. (color $ name) .or. (age < size)

    i. (lower(color) $ name)

   *j. (age < 25)

    k. (name = 'Fred') .and. (size > 40)

*5. What commands would you use to print a list of all raw material items in which Chez Jacques has more than $50.00 invested? The list should not include record numbers or field names. Remember that investment in inventory is the product of unit cost and quantity on hand.

*6. When may you use the = sign when comparing strings, and when must the $ operator be used?

DOCUMENTATION RESEARCH

Using the reference manual, determine the answer to the following questions which deal with the commands and functions discussed in this Unit. I recommend you also write the page number by the discussion of the command or function, above.

1. ? command -- what will a single ? without a following {expression} do?

2. AT(char string 1,char string 2) -- what value will be returned if char string 1 is not contained in char string 2?

3. CHR(numeric expression) -- what numeric expression will sound the "bell"?

4. How are the LEN(char string) and TRIM(char string) functions combined to determine the number of characters in a character type database field?

5. STR(numeric expression,length,decimals) -- what will happen if the length is less than the number of digits in the number?

Unit

5 SUMMARY STATISTICS

dBASE provides commands which compute summary statistics about all or a specified portion of the numeric fields in the data file. The purpose of this short unit is to introduce you to these commands.

LEARNING OBJECTIVE

At the completion of this unit you should be able to use each of the summary statistics commands.

IMPORTANT COMMANDS

COUNT
SUM
AVERAGE

COUNTS

The COUNT command counts the number of records in the file or a selected portion of the file. The result of the command COUNT is the number of records in the file. *COUNT does not add up (i.e., sum) the contents of the fields.* To count the number of records for which a given {condition} is true, use the form

COUNT FOR {condition}

COUNT is usually used with a logical {condition}. For instance, COUNT FOR (STATE='ND') will tell you how many people in your mailing list live in North Dakota, while COUNT FOR .NOT.(STATE='NY') will tell you how many live in places other than New York.

SUMS

The SUM command computes the sum of the values of numeric fields and formulas in the file or a selected portion of the file. The sums are printed on the screen and may be stored in memory variables. The common forms of the command are

SUM	*sums all numeric fields in all records*
SUM {list}	*sums listed fields and formulas for all records*
SUM FOR {condition}	*sums only those records for which {condition} is true*
SUM {list} FOR {condition}	*sums fields and formulas in records for which {condition} is true*

The {list} may be composed of field names or formulas. For instance, if you have a personnel file with hours worked and hourly rate in fields HOURS and RATE, you could use the command SUM HOURS, HOURS*RATE to yield the number of hours worked as well as the total wages earned.

AVERAGES

The AVERAGE command computes the arithmetic mean of all or a subset of numeric fields.* It is similar in form to the SUM command:

AVERAGE	*averages all numeric fields in all records*
AVERAGE {list}	*averages listed fields and formulas for all records*
AVERAGE FOR {condition}	*averages only those records for which {condition} is true*
AVERAGE {list} FOR {condition}	*averages fields and formulas in records for which {condition} is true*

EXAMPLES

Examples of the use of the statistics commands are illustrated in Figure 5-1. First, the file RAW_MATL was opened with the USE command. Then COUNT determines the total number of records in the file. The second count tells us that six records have an inventory in excess of 500.

SUM, without any logical condition, sums all numeric fields (two in this case) and displays the results. The second sum command is more selective -- only those items for which the cost is greater than .07 are chosen. Note that the second command sums a computed expression, not individual fields.

---

* This command is not available in dBASE II.

```
. use raw_matl
. count
     19 records
. count for (inventory>500)
      6 records
. sum
     19 records summed
        COST      INVENTORY
        1.05          8784
. sum cost*inventory for (cost>.07)
      5 records summed
     cost*inventory
           161.36
. sum cost*inventory for '(oz.)'$desc
      6 records summed
     cost*inventory
           156.99
. average
     19 records averaged
     COST INVENTORY
     0.06      462
. average cost*inventory
     19 records averaged
cost*inventory
        21.79
. average cost*inventory for 'cup'$lower(desc)
      3 records averaged
 cost*inventory
         13.67

.  _
```

FIGURE 5-1 Illustration of the Summary Statistics Commands
Note: Items entered by the user are in **Boldface**

The third sum command computes the sum for those records which have "(oz.)" in the description field. Again, the sum computed is a computed expression composed of two numeric fields, and not the sum of the fields.

The first AVERAGE command simply averages all numeric fields for all records. In the second instance, the average is of a computed expression. In the final case, only certain records are included in the average.

GUIDED ACTIVITY

This activity requires you to use the summary statistics commands. Before you go to the lab to work on this activity, you should answer the Review Questions for this Unit. The results of using similar commands are illustrated in Figure 5-1.

1. Follow the startup procedure for your version of dBASE as outlined in Unit 2.

2. Compute the following:

✔CHECKPOINT

What command must you give before you can answer the following questions about the finished goods (menu) file?

_____

   a. the number of Chez Jacques menu items which sell for less than 1.00.

   b. the average selling price of the menu items. (The average selling price is probably a meaningless figure, but compute it anyway.)

✔CHECKPOINT

What command must you give before you can answer the following questions about the raw materials file?

_____

   c. the total inventory value of raw materials. (Inventory value is defined as the product of quantity on hand and cost per unit.)

   d. the inventory value of raw materials which are measured by the ounce.

   e. the inventory value of raw materials which are not measured by the ounce.

3. When you have completed all of the above, give the command QUIT to exit dBASE. If everything is proper, turn off the computer and return the dBASE software to the Lab Supervisor.

REVIEW QUESTIONS

What command(s) would you use to

*1. count the number of Chez Jacques menu items which sell for less than 1.00?

2. compute the average selling price of the menu items? (The average selling price is probably a meaningless figure, but compute it anyway.)

*3. compute the total inventory value of raw materials? (Inventory value is defined as the product of quantity on hand and cost per unit.)

4. compute the inventory value of raw materials which are measured by the ounce?

*5. compute the inventory value of raw materials which are not stored by the ounce?

DOCUMENTATION RESEARCH

Using the reference manual, determine the answer to the following questions which deal with the commands discussed in this Unit. I recommend you also write the page number by the discussion of the command, above.

1. COUNT -- how can you avoid counting all records in the active database?

2. SUM -- how can you avoid summing all fields of all records in the active database?

3. AVERAGE -- how can you avoid averaging all fields of all records in the active database?

Unit

6 DATA FILE ORDER AND SEARCH

This unit deals with commands which allow you to specify the order in which data is presented and which allow you to search the data file for records with specific values in one or more fields. These are some of the most important DBMS commands.

With these commands, you will be able to determine ordinal position (e.g., who is first?, who is third?), have your output appear in a certain order (e.g., in zip code order, alphabetical) regardless of the order it was input, quickly find a specific record (e.g., how many hamburger patties do we have?), or locate and process records which meet a criterion (e.g., all materials inventoried by the ounce).

LEARNING OBJECTIVES

1. At the completion of this unit you should know

   a. what the record pointer and current record are,

   b. the difference between sorting and indexing,

   c. what ASCII collating sequence means,

   d. the difference between finding and locating.

2. At the completion of this unit you should be able to

   a. sort a file,

   b. index a file,

   c. find a record,

   d. locate records.

61

IMPORTANT COMMANDS

SORT TO {file} ON {field}
INDEX ON {expression} TO {index file name}
USE {data file name} INDEX {index file name}
REINDEX
GO TOP
GO BOTTOM
FIND {char string}
LOCATE FOR {condition}
CONTINUE

ORDERING THE DATA IN A FILE

There are two methods for arranging the data in a file in some specific order. One, SORT, physically rearranges the data; the other, INDEX, builds a table of pointers which makes the data appear to have been rearranged. Although there are advantages to having a sorted file, you will generally use the index capability because indexing takes less time and is more flexible. Indexing can also be a first step in sorting, as discussed below.

Sorting

The SORT command is used to create a new file which is a reordered copy of the file in use. The records in the new file may be in either ascending or descending order. Ascending is the default, to achieve descending order (i.e., Z->A, 9->0) type /D after {field}. The file in use remains unaltered.

The general form of the SORT command is

SORT TO {file} ON {field}

where {file} is any legitimate filename and {field} is the field name of any one field in the database being sorted.* If {field} is character type, then ASCII collating sequence is used (cf., Table 6-1). Therefore, Smith will follow SMITH and SMYTHE, de Smet will follow all of them, and 3D Cinema will precede all.

As a result of the sort operation, you will have two files with identical records, but the records will be in different order. You must USE the file you created by sorting before you will see the effect of the sorting.

Sorting is useful when you want to permanently alter the order of a file, and that order can be defined by one or more fields.** A sorted file can be read from beginning to end faster than an indexed file. On the other hand, sorting takes more time, uses more disk space, and is less flexible than indexing.

---

* In dBASE II, the general form is SORT ON {field} TO {file}
** Only one field at a time may be sorted with dBASE II, multiple fields are permitted in dBASE III.

TABLE 6-1 ASCII Collating Sequence
(printable characters only)

<space>	0	@	P	'	p
!	1	A	Q	a	q
"	2	B	R	b	r
#	3	C	S	c	s
$	4	D	T	d	t
%	5	E	U	e	u
&	6	F	V	f	v
'	7	G	W	g	w
(	8	H	X	h	x
)	9	I	Y	i	y
*	:	J	Z	j	z
+	;	K	[	k	{
,	<	L	\	l	|
-	=	M	]	m	}
.	>	N	^	n	~
/	?	O	_	o	

Note: ascending order proceeds down column, from left to right, i.e., ? precedes @

Indexing

The INDEX command is used to create an index file (with an .NDX extension) which contains pointers to records in the file currently in use. After indexing, the file appears to be sorted in ascending order of key values, but is not changed.

The general form of the INDEX command is

INDEX ON {expression} TO {index filename}

where {index filename} is a legitimate filename and {expression} is a dBASE expression formed of field names, operators and functions. To keep life simple in those situations when there is one primary key in a file, I usually name the index file the same as the data file, e.g., INDEX ON STOCKS TO STOCKS will create a STOCKS.NDX to go along with my STOCKS.DBF .

Key Expressions. The data in the {expression} may be Character, Numeric, or Date type. With INDEX, more than one field of the same type may be used to comprise the {expression} -- the index key. Index keys are computed expressions, not logical conditions.

If {expression} is character type, then ASCII collating sequence is used. Therefore, Smith will follow SMITH and SMYTHE, and de Smet will follow all of them. To overcome this problem, key on UPPER({expression}) [converting the key expression to all upper case characters]. This solution works for INDEX, but not for SORT. For example, if NAME is the name of a character field, then INDEX ON UPPER(NAME) TO INDXFILE would place Machinery between MacHenry and MacIlvenna instead of after them. This operation does not change the original file fields to MACHENRY, MACHINERY, and MACILVENNA, the original data in the file stays as it was. The effect of the expression is only on the index key, not on the original data.

The {expression} may also be formed by the concatenation of two or more character fields. For instance, an {expression} such as upper(last_name)+upper(first_name) would arrange a file of names in typical alphabetical order.

In some cases, you wish to index numeric type data in descending order. If NUMBER is the name of a numeric field, INDEX ON NUMBER TO STOCKS will create an index in lowest to highest order, while INDEX ON -1*NUMBER TO STOCKS will create an index in highest to lowest order of NUMBER field values.

The {expression} may also be formed as a function of two or more numeric fields. For instance, an {expression} such as GRADEPTS/HOURS would arrange a file of student information in ascending GPA order.

Opening a Previously Indexed File. Once indexed, the file will continue to be accessed in key order until closed (by CLEAR ALL or USE ...). In later sessions, reopen the file with the command

USE {data filename} INDEX {index filename}

A file need be indexed only once if all subsequent uses of that file include the INDEX parameter. APPEND, EDIT, REPLACE, and many other commands will automatically update the index file. It is possible to create multiple indexes (via several INDEX commands) all of which will be updated by APPEND, etc. The USE command should be as follows:

USE {file} INDEX {index1}, {index2}, ... , {index7}

In this case, only {index1} affects the apparent order of the records, but {index2} ... {index7} will be updated by changes to their respective keys.

Rebuilding an Index. Most of us will forget on occasion to include the INDEX parameter when we use a file. If we make changes to the key field of the file, the index will probably become useless. dBASE has a command called REINDEX which will rebuild all active indexes.

To use this command, USE the data file with relevant indexes, USE FILE INDEX INDEX1, INDEX2 , then issue the command REINDEX . REINDEX will read each index file to see what the key expression is, then perform the index operation again using the data file as it now exists.

The Index/Sort. If you have a large indexed file on a floppy disk, you will notice that sequential access of indexed records takes some time. To speed up the process, you may want to "index/sort" that file. The procedure is as follows:

```
use bigfile
index on name to bigindex          Creates BIGINDEX.NDX
copy to bigsort                    Records are copied to BIGSORT.DBF in NAME-order
use bigfile                        Without index
delete all                         These two commands remove all records
pack                                   from BIGFILE.DBF, see Unit 8
append from bigsort                Records are appended, now in NAME-order
index on name to bigindex          Creates BIGINDEX.NDX for subsequent work
```

Make sure you have a backup copy of BIGFILE.DBF before trying this one.

Temporary Indexes. On some occasions, you may wish to make an ad hoc inquiry, i.e., an inquiry designed to answer a specific question. For instance, you may need to determine which is the most expensive raw material. The easiest way to answer this question is to arrange the data in order from lowest to highest COST, then list the file to see what is the last record.

To accomplish such an operation, I usually build a temporary index, one which is used only for the moment and will not be maintained. To answer the question posed above using the RAW_MATL file, the sequence is as follows:

```
use raw_matl
index on cost to temp
list
use raw_matl index raw_matl
```

The first command opens the RAW_MATL.DBF file. In the second command, an index file named TEMP.NDX is created. I always use the name TEMP for temporary index files so I know that they are temporary. In TEMP.NDX, the record pointers will be in ascending order of the COST field, thus the highest cost will be last. The list command shows me the entire data file with, of course, the highest cost being the last record displayed. I make a note to myself of what the highest cost raw material is, then, with the last command, re-open the file with its permanent index (which you will build in Application B).

dBASE III has a feature called safety which is designed to protect you from inadvertent erasing of a file.* If you have done this procedure before, and a file called TEMP.NDX appears on the disk, dBASE III will ask you

TEMP.NDX already exists, overwrite (Y/N)?

before it destroys the old TEMP.NDX . In this case, it is safe to answer Y because the old file is no longer needed.

Benefits of Indexing. Indexing a file does two very useful things. First, the file will appear to be in index key order during operations such as list and when writing reports. Second, you can quickly find a particular key value in an indexed file (the topic of the next section). Although sorting the file will yield the first benefit, indexing is faster and more flexible because it permits multiple fields in the key expression.

---

* Safety is not implemented in dBASE II

SEARCHING THROUGH A FILE

There are two methods for searching through a data file. If the file is indexed and the key is unique for each record, then FIND is extremely fast, even on large floppy disk data files. If the file is not indexed, or if the key is not unique, then LOCATE must be used.

The Record Pointer

With the exception of APPEND and EDIT commands, we have not been concerned with the contents of a specific record, but rather with all records or a group of records that match a criterion (such as the LIST FOR ... examples). The reason for a file search, however, is often to locate a specific record which will be displayed, edited, or used in a computation.

When a file is first used without an index, dBASE will point at the first physical record -- the first record you entered after the APPEND command. When a file is first used with an index, dBASE will point at the first record in index-key order, which is the first logical record. As you move through the file by searching for specific records, the record pointer also moves. Unlike most computer languages, you do not need an explicit command (such as "input") to read data from the file, moving the record pointer to a record automatically reads the contents of each of the fields of the record. The record at which the record pointer is pointing is called the current record.

For the moment, we will use the DISPLAY command to show us what is in the current record. In later sections, you will learn how to perform computations on current record data.

The First or Last Record

If we are interested in viewing the data in the first or last record we may use the commands GO TOP and GO BOTTOM . If the file is indexed, then the first record will be the record with the lowest value of the index key, while the last record will have the highest value of the index key.

This capability is especially useful when we want to know the extreme values, such as "most costly" or "least quantity" in our data. We index on the value of interest, then go to the top or bottom of the file to find the record with the extreme value.

Finding a Particular Record

The FIND command causes dBASE to find the first record in the indexed data file in use whose key is the same as {char string}. FIND will work only if the data file has been indexed and opened (with the USE command) with the index.

The general form of the FIND command is

FIND {char string}

```
. use raw_matl
. index on rmid to raw_matl
     19 records indexed
. go top
. display next 10
Record#   RMID DESC              COST INVENTORY LAST_ORDER
      8   0001 all-beef patty    0.10       100 10/01/85
     19   0002 sp. sauce (oz.)   0.01       400 09/30/85
     15   0003 lettuce leaf      0.01        90 10/03/85
     12   0004 cheese slice      0.02       255 10/09/85
     16   0005 pickle slice      0.03       900 09/15/85
     11   0006 ch. onion (oz.)   0.06       876 10/10/85
     18   0007 sesame seed bun   0.12       400 10/08/85
     17   0008 regular bun       0.10       200 10/03/85
     10   0009 catsup (oz.)      0.04       386 10/10/85
     14   0010 fren. fry (oz.)   0.01       999 10/12/85
. find 0013
. display
Record#   RMID DESC              COST INVENTORY LAST_ORDER
      5   0013 8 oz. cup         0.02       600 10/06/85
. find 0030
No find

. _
```

FIGURE 6-1 Illustration of INDEX and FIND Commands
Note: Items entered by the user are in **boldface**.

where {char string} is a string of characters. The string need not be enclosed in quote marks, except when the string contains leading blanks.

If the index key is character type, then FIND will operate when given the first few characters of the key, e.g., FIND Ros will find Ross, unless Rosenbaum is also in the file. FIND always finds the first occurrence, regardless of where the record pointer was prior to the issuance of the command. Therefore, a second FIND Ros will still find Rosenbaum, even if Ross is the next record.

The {char string} must match the index {expression}. If you used UPPER(name) as the index {expression}, then FIND Ros will fail because all key values are in upper case. In such a situation, the {char string} would also have to be in upper case, e.g., FIND ROS , even if the data in the field itself is in upper and lower case. This is because FIND goes to the index file and searches for a match, if a match is found it refers to the record number of the match in the data file.

The text to be found must start in column 1 (the first byte) of the index key. FIND Andrew will not find McAndrew.

If there is no match, the message "No find" will be displayed on the screen.

Illustration of Index and Find

The Index and Find commands are illustrated in the example in Figure 6-1. First, the RAW_MATL file is opened with the Use command. Then the file is indexed with RMID as the key expression. Note that dBASE tells us how many records are indexed.

We move to the first record of the file with GO TOP, then display the next ten records. Recall that DISPLAY NEXT shows the current record as the first of the records. In this case, the records with RMIDs of 0001 through 0010 are displayed. The physical record numbers are also displayed in the left column, which provides a reference should we need to edit one of the records.

The next command is FIND 0013 which will move the record pointer to the first record which has the index key of 0013. We use the DISPLAY command to view the contents of the record. Finally, when we attempt to FIND 0030, we discover that there is no record with that RMID (i.e., index key) in our file and are presented with a "No find" message.

Locating Records

The LOCATE FOR and CONTINUE commands are used to locate records in which {condition} is true. The general form of the commands is

LOCATE FOR {condition}
    other dBASE commands
CONTINUE

LOCATE starts at the first record and searches forward from that record. When the record for which the logical {condition} is true is found, the message "Record = n" is displayed.

The located record may be processed (*other dBASE commands*). Then the next record in which {condition} is true may be found with the CONTINUE command. CONTINUE, in effect, means "perform the last LOCATE command, starting with the record after the current record."

LOCATE works faster in a file used without an index, but may be used whether or not the file is indexed.

You may be wondering when you would ever use the LOCATE command. One instance would be when you wish to find a record which meets a specific criterion, but that criterion may not be suitable as an index key. Also, LOCATE...CONTINUE is necessary if you wish to find more than the first occurrence of the criterion.

For instance, you may wish to locate all people who live in cities with "Bay" in the address (Coos Bay, Whitefish Bay, Bay City, Bayview). If you indexed the file on CITY (assuming that you have a field named CITY in the data file), you would be able to find only the first Bay (Bay City). If you were to use the LOCATE command LOCATE FOR ('Bay'$city) , the first occurrence of "Bay" in a CITY field would be located, and dBASE would respond "Record = n." You could then do whatever you wanted with that record, perhaps editing it, then give the CONTINUE command to find the next "Bay."

```
. use raw_matl
. go top
. display next 10
Record#   RMID DESC               COST INVENTORY LAST_ORDER
      1   0014 12 oz. cup         0.03       300 10/04/85
      2   0015 16 oz. cup         0.05       400 09/28/85
      3   0018 4 oz. fry pack     0.02       332 10/19/85
      4   0019 6 oz. fry pack     0.03       500 10/15/85
      5   0013 8 oz. cup          0.02       600 10/06/85
      6   0011 Coca Cola (oz.)    0.05       800 10/13/85
      7   0012 Sprite (oz.)       0.05       700 10/12/85
      8   0001 all-beef patty     0.10       100 10/01/85
      9   0016 apple pie          0.16       346 08/15/85
     10   0009 catsup (oz.)       0.04       386 10/10/85
. locate for 'cup'$desc
Record =          1
. display
Record#   RMID DESC               COST INVENTORY LAST_ORDER
      1   0014 12 oz. cup         0.03       300 10/04/85
. continue
Record =          2
. display
Record#   RMID DESC               COST INVENTORY LAST_ORDER
      2   0015 16 oz. cup         0.05       400 09/28/85
. continue
Record =          5
. display
Record#   RMID DESC               COST INVENTORY LAST_ORDER
      5   0013 8 oz. cup          0.02       600 10/06/85
. continue
End of locate scope

. _
```

FIGURE 6-2 Illustration of LOCATE and CONTINUE Commands
Note: Items entered by the user are in **boldface**.

If you wish to search only a portion of your data file, LOCATE may be limited to a certain scope by specifying the range of records to be searched, for example

locate next 5 for ('Bay'$city)

in which case the command starts with the current record, not the beginning of the file.

Illustration of Locate and Continue

Use of the LOCATE command is illustrated in Figure 6-2. In this case, we wish to find all the cups in our inventory list. Since the word "cup" is not the first word in the description field, we are not able to use the FIND command. Another reason for using the locate command is that find will find only one occurrence, and we must locate all occurrences of the word.

The first command opens the file, without index. The DISPLAY NEXT 10 command shows the first ten records, but leaves the record pointer at record number 1.

LOCATE FOR 'cup'$DESC yields the response "Record =   1" telling us that dBASE has found a match. The record is displayed, then the CONTINUE command is used to find succeeding matches. The response "End of locate scope" after the last CONTINUE tells us that we have found all that are in the data file.

GUIDED ACTIVITY

This activity required you to duplicate the illustrations used in this unit.

1. Follow the startup procedure for your version of dBASE as outlined in Unit 2.

2. Duplicate the instructions in **boldface** type in Figure 6-1. Your screen should look like that figure as you progress through the exercise.

3. Duplicate the instructions in **boldface** type in Figure 6-2. Your screen should look like that figure as you progress through the exercise.

4. Now give the command USE RAW_MATL INDEX RAW_MATL

5. Give the command LOCATE FOR 'cup'$DESC

✔ CHECKPOINT
Which record is found first? Why?

_____

6. Use the CONTINUE command to find the other two records with "cup" in the DESC field.

7. Experiment further with FIND and LOCATE, for instance you may wish to locate all raw materials which are buns.

8. When you are finished, use the QUIT command to exit dBASE. Remember to backup your work and return all materials to the Lab Supervisor.

REVIEW QUESTIONS

1. What is the difference between indexing and sorting? Which creates another .DBF file? Which creates an .NDX file?

2. Indexing provides two benefits, what are they?

*3. What command would you use to index the file RAW_MATL on the field RMID, creating the file RAW_MATL.NDX (cf., Application A)?

4. Define each of the following terms:

   a. current record

   *b. physical record order

   *c. logical record

   d. record pointer

5. Assume that you have indexed RAW_MATL as suggested in question 3.

   *a. What command will take you directly to the record with RMID field of 0010?

   b. Refer to Table 1-1. What command will take you to the apple pie record?

6. How you you know if

   *a. a FIND has been successful?

   *b. a FIND has not been successful?

   *c. a LOCATE has been successful?

   *d. a LOCATE has not been successful?

7. What commands would you use to determine the most expensive item on the Chez Jacques menu (finished goods file)?

8. Jacques wants you to change his menu, replacing the English word "Pie" with the French word "Tarte" in all relevant records. What commands will you use to locate the first occurrence of "Pie" in the DESC field, edit the record, then proceed to the next occurrence.

*9. Both LOCATE ... CONTINUE and LIST FOR ... commands can be used to discover all records in a data file which match a certain logical condition. When would you need to use LOCATE, and when would LIST be sufficient?

DOCUMENTATION RESEARCH

Using the reference manual, determine the answer to the following questions which deal with the commands discussed in this Unit. I recommend you also write the page number by the discussion of the command, above.

1. SORT TO {file} ON {field} -- how can multiple fields be included in the sort key (dBASE III) or how do you sort on multiple fields (dBASE II)?

2. INDEX ON {expression} TO {index file name} -- how can numeric and date fields be combined with character fields into the key {expression}?

3. INDEX ON {expression} TO {index file name} -- what is the maximum length of the key {expression}?

4. REINDEX -- which index file(s) is(are) rebuilt by this command?

5. GO TOP -- what effect does an index in use have on this command?

6. GO BOTTOM -- what effect does an index in use have on this command?

7. FIND {char string} -- what must you do if the search key {char string} includes leading blanks?

8. LOCATE FOR {condition} -- how do you force this command to start the search at the current record?

9. CONTINUE -- if the LOCATE command is limited with a {scope}, how does this command use the original {scope}?

Application

B CHEZ JACQUES (II)

This application exercise requires you to use the data ordering and file searching commands in a data file.

1. Follow the startup procedure for your version of dBASE as outlined in Unit 2.

2. Put the disk containing files RAW_MATL.DBF, MIX.DBF, and FIN_GOOD.DBF in drive B (or the only drive in a fixed disk PC).

3. Index the file FIN_GOOD using FGID as the key and creating the file FIN_GOOD.NDX Note: the file must be used before it can be indexed.

4. Next, index the file RAW_MATL using RMID as the key and creating RAW_MATL.NDX

5. Finally, index the file MIX, using FGID as the key and creating the file MIX.NDX

6. USE FIN_GOOD INDEX FIN_GOOD

7. FIND the record which has FGID of 1011. Use the DISPLAY command to show you what item that is. Do the same for item 1001. Do a screen print to capture this moment forever.

8. Determine the most expensive item on the Chez Jacques menu. Do a screen print to show the commands you used.

9. Change the Chez Jacques menu, replacing the English word "Pie" with the French word "Tarte" in all relevant records. The LOCATE ... CONTINUE commands may help.

10. When you have completed all of the above, give the command QUIT to exit dBASE. If everything is proper, turn off the computer and return the dBASE software to the Lab Supervisor.

7 OPERATING PARAMETERS AND DISK FILES

This unit is devoted to a discussion of commands which deal with disk file storage and the operating environment of dBASE. As you become a more advanced dBASE user, you will learn how to use these commands to make your work easier.

LEARNING OBJECTIVES

1. At the completion of this unit you should know

    a. how to identify the purpose a file serves by the file extension,

    b. the purpose of the various operating parameters and how to alter those parameters.

2. At the completion of this unit you should be able to

    a. obtain a directory of data files on a disk,

    b. obtain a directory of all files on a disk,

    c. obtain a directory of all files of a certain type,

    d. copy all or a portion of a data file to another data file,

    e. copy all or a portion of a data file to a file suitable for importation into a spreadsheet or word processing program,

    f. display the current settings of function keys,

    g. change the current settings of function keys.

IMPORTANT COMMANDS

DISPLAY STATUS
SET DEFAULT TO {drive}
SET PRINT ON/OFF
SET FUNCTION {number} TO {character string}
COPY TO {filename}
COPY FILE {source} TO {target}
TYPE
DIR
ERASE {filename}
RENAME {filename}
APPEND FROM {filename}

OPERATING PARAMETERS

It is possible to change many of the operating parameters of dBASE, such as screen appearance and the commands issued by the function keys. This section is concerned with a version of the DISPLAY command which shows you what the parameters are and with the SET command which allows you to change those parameters.

Displaying Parameters

The DISPLAY STATUS command is used to provide a summary of the current operating status. The command will list any open databases and their indexes as well as the current settings of all SET commands (see below). This command is illustrated in Figure 7-1.

In dBASE III, you may use DISPLAY STATUS TO PRINT to obtain a printed copy.*

LIST STATUS will also display operating status, but does not pause after filling the screen with information.

The DISPLAY STATUS command may be given by typing the F6 key.

Changing Parameters

The SET command allows many operating parameters to be changed. In dBASE II there are 28 versions of the SET command, while in dBASE III there are 35 possibilities. Rather than write a book on the various options, we will discuss a few of the most useful here and refer to others in later units as appropriate. Table 7-1 contains a list of all SET commands for your future reference.

---

* In dBASE II, you will have to toggle the printer on and off with SET PRINT ON and OFF to obtain a printed copy.

```
.  display status

Currently selected database:
Select area -  1, Database in use: B:billing.dbf    Alias - BILLING
       Index file: B:billing.ndx  key - org_code

Press any key to continue...

File search path:
Default disk drive: B:
ALTERNATE   - OFF  DEBUG      - OFF  ESCAPE     - ON   MENU      - OFF
BELL        - ON   DELETED    - OFF  EXACT      - OFF  PRINT     - OFF
CARRY       - OFF  DELIMITERS - OFF  HEADING    - ON   SAFETY    - ON
CONFIRM     - OFF  DEVICE     - SCRN HELP       - ON   STEP      - OFF
CONSOLE     - ON   ECHO       - OFF  INTENSITY  - ON   TALK      - ON
UNIQUE      - OFF


Margin =      0

Function key  F1  - help;
Function key  F2  - assist;
Function key  F3  - list;
Function key  F4  - dir;
Function key  F5  - display structure;
Function key  F6  - display status;
Function key  F7  - display memory;
Function key  F8  - display;
Function key  F9  - append;
Function key  F10 - edit;

.  _
```

FIGURE 7-1 Illustration of the DISPLAY STATUS Command
Note: Item entered by the user is in **boldface**

Default Disk Drive. The default disk drive is where dBASE will store a file you create
and look for a file you open. The SET DEFAULT command tells dBASE which drive to use.
It is generally mandatory with dBASE II, and may be necessary with dBASE III, to give the
command SET DEFAULT TO B: so that your files go to your disk rather than the program
disk. (With a fixed disk PC, SET DEFAULT TO A: .)

If you are using dBASE III, the person responsible for the software should have created a
file on the System disk (i.e., the disk in drive A: or the hard disk) named CONFIG.DB
which accomplishes this automatically. If the file does not exist, you must remember to
type SET DEFAULT TO B: (or A:) each time you start dBASE.

TABLE 7-1 SET Commands

SET ...	Function
ALTERNATE ON/**OFF**	records all keyboard entries and screen displays in an output file for later reference
ALTERNATE TO ...	names the output file
BELL **ON**/OFF	bell sounds when input data fills field
CARRY ON/**OFF**	data from previous record is copied to new record during APPEND
COLON **ON**/OFF**	same as SET DELIMITER ON/**OFF**
COLOR TO ...	changes colors or screen attributes
CONFIRM ON/**OFF**	controls whether or not input skips to next field when current field is full during APPEND and EDIT
CONSOLE **ON**/OFF	turns video display on and off
DATE TO ...**	resets internal date
DEBUG ON/**OFF**	used to locate errors in programs
DECIMALS TO ...*	controls number of decimal places displayed
DEFAULT TO ...	changes default drive for file operations
DELETED ON/**OFF**	determines whether records marked for deletion are considered by other commands
DELIMITER ON/**OFF***	sets method of marking field widths for APPEND and EDIT
DELIMITER TO ...*	defines character(s) for delimiting
DEVICE TO ...*	routes @ command output to screen or printer -- in dBASE II, part of the SET FORMAT TO ... command
ECHO ON/**OFF**	controls whether or not command lines from programs are displayed on the screen
EJECT **ON**/OFF**	controls initial page eject in REPORT command
ESCAPE **ON**/OFF	determines whether or not an Esc will abort commands
EXACT ON/**OFF**	affects character string equivalence in {conditions}
FILTER TO ...*	only records which meet a condition will be available
FIXED ON/**OFF***	all numeric output displays same number of decimal places
FORMAT TO ...	selects customized format
FUNCTION ...	reprograms function keys, in dBASE II, SET F{n}
HEADING **ON**/OFF*	controls display of column titles with DISPLAY and LIST
HEADING TO ...**	REPORT heading line
HELP **ON**/OFF*	turns help query on and off
INDEX TO ...	opens index files, alternative to USE ... INDEX command
INTENSITY **ON**/OFF	determines display of fields for APPEND and EDIT
LINKAGE ON/**OFF****	controls movement of primary and secondary files
MARGIN TO ...	sets left margin for printed output
MENUS **ON**/OFF*	displays a cursor key menu when appropriate
PATH TO ...*	sets path to be searched for files (PC-DOS 2.0 and later)
PRINT ON/**OFF**	directs output to printer as well as screen
PROCEDURE TO ...*	opens a procedure file (similar to a set of subroutines)
RAW ON/**OFF****	controls spacing between fields in DISPLAY and LIST commands
RELATION TO ...*	links two files (see Part Three of this manual)
SAFETY **ON**/OFF*	provides protection against inadvertent erasing of files
SCREEN **ON**/OFF**	turns full-screen operations on and off
STEP ON/**OFF**	used to cause program to execute a step at a time
TALK **ON**/OFF	causes response to commands to be displayed
UNIQUE ON/**OFF***	used with INDEX to eliminate records with duplicate keys

Notes: default settings are in **boldface**
   * not available, dBASE II   ** not available, dBASE III

TABLE 7-2 Function Key Assignments

dBASE III

F1	Help;	F2	Assist;
F3	List;	F4	Dir;
F5	Display Structure;	F6	Display Status;
F7	Display Memory;	F8	Display;
F9	Append;	F10	Edit;

dBASE II

F1	Help;	F2	Disp;
F3	List;	F4	List Files;
F5	List Stru;	F6	List Status;
F7	List Memo;	F8	Create;
F9	Append;	F10	Edit #;

Printer Toggle. Most versions of dBASE allow you to toggle the printer on and off with the SET PRINT command. After SET PRINT ON , almost all screen output will be sent to the printer as well as to the screen. Use SET PRINT OFF to stop the effect.

Function Keys. The 10 IBM PC function keys have been assigned useful commands, which appear in Table 7-2. If you wish to change the default setting, use the SET FUNCTION** command:

SET FUNCTION {number} TO {character string}

where {number} is the number of the key to be reassigned and {character string} is the command that pressing the key should produce. The {character string} may include up to 30 characters, including spaces. The {character string} should include a ; (semicolon) wherever the <CR> key should be pressed. More than one command may be assigned to a function key, within the 30 character limit. Function key F1 can not be reassigned.

Examples:

    set function 4 to 'use raw__matl;'
    set function 7 to 'set print on;list;
    set function 8 to 'eject;set print off;'

The default function key assignments may be changed via the CONFIG.DB file. Again, this is the task of the person responsible for the software, not the individual user.

---

* In early versions of dBASE II, you may have to use Ctrl-P or Ctrl-PrtSc to accomplish the on/off toggle.
** This command is not available in some versions of dBASE II, where available, it is SET F{number} TO {character string} , e.g., SET F4 TO 'USE RAW_MATL;'

DISK FILES

This section deals with the storage of files on disks. Most PC-DOS application programs, including dBASE, use the file extension to designate the purpose the file serves, i.e., the file type. If you are not familiar with the general rules for file names and extensions, refer to the appendix to this manual.

Some of the commands already discussed deal with disk files. For instance, CREATE and INDEX create files on the disk. APPEND adds data to a data file. USE opens a disk file for reading or writing. The commands discussed below complement those commands already presented.

File Type

dBASE creates several types of files, each with a unique file extension:

Type of File	Extension
database	.DBF
database memo	.DBT
index	.NDX
memory	.MEM
command	.PRG
format	.FMT
label	.LBL
report form	.FRM
text output	.TXT

These are discussed as necessary throughout this manual.

Copying Files

Database to Database Copies. The COPY command duplicates all or part of the open file in another file. The general form is

COPY TO {filename}

where {filename} is any legal filename. A .DBF extension is added automatically. The copy operation may be limited to a certain {field list} or to records which meet a logical {condition}:

COPY TO {filename} FIELDS {field list}

COPY TO {filename} FOR {condition}

COPY TO {filename} FIELDS {field list} FOR {condition}

```
. dir
Database files      # records      last update      size
ACCOUNTS.DBF            308         06/09/85        21504
BILLING.DBF             57          06/05/85         6094
CASHFLOW.DBF            301         02/24/85        18460
CRTOT.DBF               27          02/24/85         1024
DRTOT.DBF               56          02/24/85         1536
TIME_LOG.DBF        dBASE 2.4 database              16896
TRANSACT.DBF            2291        06/09/85       159137


  224651 bytes in        7 files.
  104448 bytes remaining on drive.
.  _
```

FIGURE 7-2 Illustration of the DIR Command
Note: Item entered by the user is in **boldface**

Examples:

      copy to backup
      copy to ages fields name, age
      copy to vip for salary > 100000
      copy to prospect fields name, address for income > 50000

Database to Text File Copies. COPY can also be used to copy all or a portion of the open file to a text file for inclusion into a word processor, spreadsheet, or other data base manager. See the section "Output to Other Applications Software" below.

Copy of Any File. The COPY FILE command creates a copy of any disk file.* The format is

      COPY FILE {source filename.ext} TO {target filename.ext}

This command performs the same function as the PC-DOS COPY command.

Directory of Files

The DIR command in dBASE III provides a list of database files (.DBF extension) on the default disk.** The output (see Figure 7-2 for an example) includes the size of the file, number of records, and date of last update, except that information on currently open files may not reflect changes since the file was opened.

---
* This command is not available in all versions of dBASE II.
** In dBASE II, the command is DISPLAY FILES or LIST FILES .

The DIR command may be given by pressing the F4 key.

You may specify a specific file name, and you may also use the ? and * wildcard characters to look for specific types of files. Examples:

    dir *.txt
    dir c:*.ndx

Erasing Files

The ERASE command in dBASE III deletes a file on the disk.* Do not erase from within dBASE unless you need the space on disk or you have a well-developed and debugged program. It is much better to erase files at PC-DOS level. Example:

    erase temp.ndx

Renaming Files

The RENAME command does what it says. Same cautions as ERASE above. Example:

    rename temp.ndx to old.ndx

OUTPUT TO OTHER APPLICATIONS SOFTWARE

The COPY command may be used to extract data from the data file which will be used by a word processing program (such as WordStar MailMerge) in form letters and other applications. This command can also extract data for further analysis by a spreadsheet program such as Lotus 1-2-3 or for input to a programming language such as BASIC.

To make the data available to other software, the output of the command must be a file in ASCII text. ASCII (American Standard Code for Information Interchange) text might also be called plain text -- it is not coded in any special way by dBASE. Most applications software can read ASCII text, so it is a good way (if not especially efficient) to move data among programs. The dBASE III command, TYPE {filename.ext}, may be used to display the contents of an ASCII file on screen or printer.

Notice, in Figure 7-3, that there are two variations of the COPY command that produce ASCII files. DELIMITED output is almost always preferred, but you may use SDF output if your applications program is written in FORTRAN or COBOL and requires structured data format.

Finally, notice how dBASE III converts date type fields for ASCII output. Your application program may or may not be able to make use of such a format.

---

* In dBASE II, the command is DELETE FILE .

```
. copy to sdf_ex for cost>.10 sdf
      3 records copied
. type sdf_ex.txt
0007sesame seed bun     0.1240019851008
0016apple pie           0.1634619850815
0017cherry pie          0.1420019850919

. copy to delim_ex.prn for cost>.10 delimited
      3 records copied
. type delim_ex.prn
"0007","sesame seed bun",0.12,400,19851008
"0016","apple pie",0.16,346,19850815
"0017","cherry pie",0.14,200,19850919


. _
```

FIGURE 7-3 Variations of the COPY Command
Note: Items entered by the user are in **boldface**

COPY TO {filename} SDF creates a file in ASCII text of the entire database. Fields are aligned similar to the output of the LIST command. This is useful when you want to include a table of data into a text document being edited by a word processor.

COPY TO {filename} DELIMITED creates a file in ASCII text of the entire database. Character type fields are enclosed in quotation marks and all fields are separated by commas.

A default extension of .TXT will be assigned unless you specify otherwise.

Lotus 1-2-3 Users: use the DELIMITED form and specify a .PRN extension --
COPY TO OUTPUT.PRN DELIMITED -- and you will be able to /FileImport without editing.

WordStar MailMerge Users: use the DELIMITED form -- COPY TO OUTPUT DELIMITED -- and you will be able to use the file as a MailMerge data file without editing.

BASIC Language Programmers: use the DELIMITED form --
COPY TO OUTPUT DELIMITED -- and you will be able to read the file as a sequential file with INPUT # statements without editing.

The output file may also be constrained using a {field list} or {condition}.

INPUT FROM OTHER APPLICATIONS SOFTWARE

The transfer of data from other applications software, such as a word processor or spreadsheet, is essentially the reverse of the process to output data to those programs. The APPEND FROM command is used, with the basic forms:

APPEND FROM {filename} DELIMITED
APPEND FROM {filename} SDF

where {filename} is a ASCII text file. dBASE assumes a .TXT file extension, but you may specify a different extension. Examples:

append from ws_file delimited
append from lot_file.prn sdf

Before appending from an another file, you must CREATE a data file to hold the incoming data. The structure you create must match the type and width of the data being imported. The receiving data file is then opened with the USE command and the appropriate version of APPEND FROM is given.

Spreadsheet Users: make sure that the type of data is the same in each column (i.e., all character or all numeric). Use the command which creates an ASCII output file (e.g., /PrintFile in Lotus 1-2-3) to put the data on a disk file. Before leaving the spreadsheet program, make careful notes of width, data type, and number of decimal places in each column. When you are in dBASE, create a file structure which matches the spreadsheet columns and use the SDF option on input. (Because some spreadsheet programs automatically assign extensions to ASCII output files, you may have to specify the extension as part of the command: APPEND FROM LOT_FILE.PRN SDF)

Word Processor Users: you may create the file with commas separating data elements and use DELIMITED form, or you may carefully align the data in columns and use SDF form.

BASIC Programmers: use the WRITE # statement which creates delimited output, then import with the DELIMITED qualifier.

GUIDED ACTIVITY

This activity requires you to use the commands discussed in this unit.

1. Follow the startup procedure for your version of dBASE as outlined in Unit 2.

2. Put the disk containing RAW_MATL.DBF, MIX.DBF, and FIN_GOOD.DBF in drive B (or the only drive on a fixed disk PC).

3. Use the DISPLAY STATUS command to see the initial system status, which will look similar to Figure 7-1. Use <SHIFT>PrtSc twice to print a copy.

4. USE RAW_MATL INDEX RAW_MATL

5. Change the meaning of function key F10 to DIR *.*

✔CHECKPOINT
What command do you use to change this function key definition?

6. SET PRINT ON

7. DISPLAY STATUS again. Did the output go to the printer? What has changed?

8. Use the COPY command to make a second copy of RAW_MATL.DBF with the name RAW2.DBF . You will see a "records copied" message similar to the one in Figure 7-3.

✔ **CHECKPOINT**
What command will you use to make this copy?

_____

9. Output a file listing all raw materials and their unit costs suitable for input into a text-merge or spreadsheet program. Again, you should see a "records copied" message similar to the one in Figure 7-3.

✔ **CHECKPOINT**
What command do you use to output a file named MERGE.TXT?

_____

10. When you have completed all of the above, give the command QUIT to exit dBASE.

11. If everything is proper, turn off the computer and return the dBASE software to the Lab Supervisor.

REVIEW QUESTIONS

1. What kind of data is contained in files with the following extensions:

   a. .DBF

   b. .TXT

   c. .NDX

2. What command will list all database files on a disk?

*3. What command will tell you what the current function key settings are?

4. What command would you use to change the meaning of function key F10 to be DIR *.* ?

5. Look at Figure 7-3. What are the characteristics of Standard Data Format and Delimited Format. What are the differences?

*6. What commands would you use to output a file listing all raw materials and their unit costs suitable for input into a text-merge or spreadsheet program?

DOCUMENTATION RESEARCH

Using the reference manual, determine the answer to the following questions which deal with the commands discussed in this Unit. I recommend you also write the page number by the discussion of the command, above.

1. DISPLAY STATUS -- what information is provided for each open database file?

2. SET DEFAULT TO {drive} -- what message will you get if the file you request is not on the defaul⁺

3. SET PRINT ON/OFF -- what could happen if you activate the printer when it is not connected or on line?

4. COPY TO {filename} -- what happens to records marked for deletion? (The concept of deleted records is discussed in the next unit.)

5. COPY FILE {source} TO {target} -- if this command is used to copy a database file with memo type fields, what else must be done?

6. DIR -- under what circumstances might this command yield incorrect information about a database file?

7. ERASE {filename} -- under what circumstances will this command not erase the file?

8. RENAME {filename} -- what must be specified if the file to be renamed is not on the default disk drive?

9. APPEND FROM {filename} -- if the DELIMITED option is used, how is the end of a field indicated?

Unit
8

DATA FILE CHANGES

This unit deals with changing data files. There are four types of changes that may be made to a data file: adding records, changing data in existing records, deleting records, and changing the data file structure.

LEARNING OBJECTIVES

1. At the completion of this unit you should know

   a. the differences among edit, change and replace commands,

   b. the various stages of the record deletion process.

2. At the completion of this unit you should be able to

   a. combine two data files,

   b. change selected fields of selected records,

   c. replace field contents on a selective basis,

   d. delete, recall, and purge records,

   e. modify the structure of a data file.

IMPORTANT COMMANDS

APPEND FROM {filename}
REPLACE {scope} {field} WITH {expression} FOR {condition}
CHANGE FIELDS {field list} FOR {condition}

```
DELETE {scope} FOR {condition}
SET DELETED ON/OFF
RECALL {scope} FOR {condition}
PACK
ZAP
DISPLAY STRUCTURE
MODIFY STRUCTURE
```

ADDING DATA FROM ANOTHER DATA FILE

The APPEND FROM command may be used to bring data from another data base (.DBF) file into the file currently open. Records marked for deletion will not be included. If the two data files have different structures, only fields that have the same structure (name and type) will be copied. This command may be used to combine the work of two or more people working on separate computers.

CHANGING DATA IN EXISTING RECORDS

There are two main reasons for changing data in existing records. The first, to correct errors of input, is best done with the EDIT command which allows you to selectively change the data in a specific record. The use of the EDIT command was discussed in Unit 3.

The second reason for changing data in existing records is to reflect changes which have taken place since the data were initially entered. For instance, all salaries may have changed as a result of the yearly budget process. Or, all employees at Boca Raton may have been transferred to Montvale. Or, someone may have gotten married and changed his name. Except where the changes affect only one record (the last instance), it is usually better to use CHANGE, BROWSE, or REPLACE commands to effect this type of change. REPLACE is best when the changes are systematic (i.e., where there is a global replacement [change all Boca Raton to Montvale] or a consistent relationship [all salaries up 10%]), while CHANGE and BROWSE are necessary when the changes are unsystematic (i.e., where there is no direct relationship between old value and new value).

Systematic Changes

The quickest way to make systematic changes is with the REPLACE command. Use this command when there is a consistent relationship between old and new values of one or more numeric fields or when any type of field is to be changed based on the contents of itself or another field. The general form of the command is

    REPLACE {scope} {field} WITH {expression} FOR {condition}

which will replace the contents of {field} with value of {expression}. Both {scope} and FOR {condition} are optional -- REPLACE will change only the current record if neither is specified. The {scope} is usually ALL which will change all records unless the FOR {condition} clause is utilized.

```
. use raw2
. replace all cost with cost*1.2
     19 records replaced
. go top
. list next 5
Record#   RMID DESC            COST  INVENTORY LAST_ORDER
        1 0014 12 oz. cup      0.04        300 10/04/85
        2 0015 16 oz. cup      0.06        400 09/28/85
        3 0018 4 oz. fry pack  0.02        332 10/19/85
        4 0019 6 oz. fry pack  0.04        500 10/15/85
        5 0013 8 oz. cup       0.02        600 10/06/85

. _
```

FIGURE 8-1 Illustration of the REPLACE Command
Note: Items entered by the user are in **boldface**

Examples:

    replace all salary with salary*1.05
        everybody gets a 5% increase

    replace salary with salary*1.1 for state='AK'
        Alaska employees get a 10% increase

    replace city with 'Montvale' for city='Boca Raton'
        I've Been Moved

The use of the Replace command is illustrated in Figure 8-1 (this is part of the Guided Activity for this unit). The file RAW2 is opened, then all costs are increased by 20%. The LIST command shows the result in the first five records.

Unsystematic Changes

There are times when the change is not systematic but the fields or records to be changed can be specified. For instance, the salary review system may yield differential pay increases based on individual performance. In this case, you must change each salary field individually, but you need to change only the salary field, not the other fields.

The CHANGE command allows you to change specific fields in a specified group of records. The general form of the command is

CHANGE FIELDS {field list} FOR {condition}

All records, or all which meet the condition of the FOR {condition} will be presented for editing. Only those fields listed will be displayed. Neither the list of fields nor the conditional condition are required, CHANGE by itself will take you through all fields of all records.

Examples:

> change fields salary,name
>> *to make individual salary adjustments; the name field is included so you will know whose salary is being changed*
>
> change for city='Mobile'
>> *to edit records of all Mobile employees*
>
> change fields salary,name for city='Mobile'
>> *combined effect of the first two examples*

The CHANGE command is available in both dBASE II and dBASE III, but the performance of the command is much improved in the latter.

The BROWSE command is one of the most amazing commands of dBASE. BROWSE displays up to 17 records on the screen at one time and you use full-screen mode to move about your data file and make changes. Those who are used to spreadsheet programs will find similarities in BROWSE. A great way to make multiple changes, also a great way to make big mistakes. Only BROWSE after you have made a backup copy of your file.

DELETING ENTIRE RECORDS

"Deleted records" in dBASE are not really "gone" -- they remain in the data file. Deletion may be used for two purposes: to make certain records temporarily "invisible" to data base inquiries without eliminating those records permanently, or as a preliminary to physical removal from the data file. The commands necessary to accomplish these are discussed in this section.

Each record in a data file has a flag character which tells dBASE whether or not the record is "deleted." (The flag character is why the total record length is one byte greater than the sum of the field widths.) "Marking a record as deleted" with the DELETE command means that the flag is set to indicate deleted, but that the record is still in the data file. The condition of the flag can be reversed, to normal or non-deleted status (by the RECALL command). Normally, dBASE will treat deleted records just like other records -- they count in sums, replaces, and so on. dBASE can be instructed to ignore those records, however, with the SET DELETED ON/OFF command. The data file may also be purged of deleted records with the PACK command.

To select just those records marked for deletion use DELETED( ), the *deleted record function.** DELETED( ) is a logical function which is true if the current record is marked for deletion, and false otherwise. Example:

---

* In dBASE II, the function is * . Example:

> display for *

```
Record No.      17                          *DEL*
RMID            0008
DESC            regular bun
COST               0.12
INVENTORY       200
LAST_ORDER      10/03/85
```

FIGURE 8-2 Editing a Deleted Record

    display for deleted( )

    When listed or displayed, an asterisk [*] appears next to the record number of
records which have been marked for deletion (illustrated in Figure 8-3). When a deleted
record is edited, *DEL* appears in the upper margin of the screen (illustrated in Figure
8-2).

Marking Records as Deleted

The DELETE command is used to mark records as deleted. The general form of the command
is

    DELETE {scope} FOR {condition}

    The command can be used to delete a specific record -- DELETE RECORD 5 --
or to delete all records that meet a condition --
DELETE FOR (SALARY > 30000).AND.(SALARY < 60000) .

    Records may also deleted during an EDIT operation. Pressing ^U (Ctrl-U) will
toggle the deleted record mark on and off for the record being edited.

Including and Ignoring Deleted Records

The SET DELETED ON/OFF command is used to inform dBASE whether or not to include
deleted records in other commands. SET DELETED is normally off, which means that
information in records marked as deleted is included in all commands. When turned on,
deleted records are ignored by all commands except INDEX and REINDEX.

Removing the Deleted Record Mark

The RECALL command changes the mark from deleted to not deleted. This command would
be used to reverse the effect of a "temporary" deletion. The general form of the command is

    RECALL {scope} FOR {condition}

Give the command SET DELETED OFF before using this command. You can use the command to recall a specific record -- RECALL RECORD 5 -- to recall all records that meet a condition -- RECALL FOR (SALARY > 30000).AND.(SALARY < 60000) -- or to recall all records -- RECALL ALL .

As mentioned above, pressing ^U during an EDIT operation will toggle the deleted record mark.

Purging Deleted Records

The PACK command purges all records marked for deletion. Prior to PACK, deleted records are present in file. After PACK, deleted records gone forever. It is wise to make a backup copy of your file before packing.

Emptying a Data File

The ZAP command removes all records from the active data file. It is the equivalent of DELETE ALL followed by PACK , but much faster. Some care is recommended.*

Examples

Two examples may clarify the use of record deletion commands. The first example uses temporary deletion, the second example uses permanent deletion.

Temporary Deletion. I keep my student grade book in a dBASE file. At the beginning of the semester, all names are entered into the file. As the semester progresses, some students will withdraw from the course. These students are assigned a 'W' in the GRADE field. I want to keep the student names and scores in the data file for future reference, but not include their scores when computing class averages. The following series of commands is used:

```
delete for grade='W'
set deleted on
average testscore
set deleted off
recall all
```

Permanent Deletion. Organizations which maintain mailing lists want to periodically purge those lists of inactive addressees. For instance, a mail-order firm may remove names of persons who have not ordered in the last two years. This would be a permanent removal. Assume that the field LAST_ORDER contains the date of last order, and that the system date is set to today's date. The following two commands would purge the file of all persons who have not ordered in the last two years:

```
delete for ((date( )-last_order)>730)
pack
```

---

* The command is not available in dBASE II.

```
. use raw2
. delete for inventory>=100
     17 records deleted
. list
Record#   RMID DESC              COST INVENTORY LAST_ORDER
      1  *0014 12 oz. cup        0.04       300 10/04/85
      2  *0015 16 oz. cup        0.06       400 09/28/85
      3  *0018 4 oz. fry pack    0.02       332 10/19/85
      4  *0019 6 oz. fry pack    0.04       500 10/15/85
      5   0013 8 oz. cup         0.02        91 10/06/85
      6  *0011 Coca Cola (oz.)   0.06       800 10/13/85
      7  *0012 Sprite (oz.)      0.06       700 10/12/85
      8  *0001 all-beef patty    0.12       100 10/01/85
      9  *0016 apple pie         0.19       346 08/15/85
     10  *0009 catsup (oz.)      0.05       386 10/10/85
     11  *0006 ch. onion (oz.)   0.07       876 10/10/85
     12  *0004 cheese slice      0.02       255 10/09/85
     13  *0017 cherry pie        0.17       200 09/19/85
     14  *0010 fren. fry (oz.)   0.01       999 10/12/85
     15   0003 lettuce leaf      0.01        90 10/03/85
     16  *0005 pickle slice      0.04       900 09/15/85
     17  *0008 regular bun       0.12       200 10/03/85
     18  *0007 sesame seed bun   0.14       400 10/08/85
     19  *0002 sp. sauce (oz.)   0.01       400 09/30/85
. set deleted on
. list
Record#   RMID DESC              COST INVENTORY LAST_ORDER
      5   0013 8 oz. cup         0.02        91 10/06/85
     15   0003 lettuce leaf      0.01        90 10/03/85
. recall all
     No records recalled
. set deleted off
. recall all
     17 records recalled

. _
```

FIGURE 8-3 Illustration of the Deleted Record Commands
Note: Items entered by the user are in **boldface**

Illustration

Chez Jacques wants a list of those raw materials for which the inventory quantity has fallen below 100 items. Although a LIST command would suffice, we will use the deleted record capabilities of dBASE. (This illustration may be found in Figure 8-3.)

The first step is to open the file RAW2. Then we use DELETE FOR INVENTORY<=100 to mark all records with more than 100 units in inventory as deleted. dBASE responds with a message indicating how many records were deleted.

The LIST command shows us which records are deleted and which are not by placing asterisks prior to the first field of those records which are marked as deleted. To obtain a list of only those records which are not marked for deletion, we SET DELETED ON and LIST again. This time, only two records are listed.

In the next command, we attempt to RECALL ALL, but no records are recalled because dBASE is ignoring all records marked as deleted. We must first SET DELETED OFF and then we may RECALL ALL.

MODIFYING THE STRUCTURE OF A DATA FILE

One of the real virtues of dBASE is that you may change your mind about the relevant data file fields and reconfigure your data file after data have been entered. It is possible to keep previously entered data, but it is also possible to erase many hours of work if you are careless. Read this section carefully.

Before the structure of a file can be modified, the file must be opened (USE command).

The general method of modifying the structure of a data file is (1) copy the contents of the file to a temporary file, (2) modify the structure of the file, (3) and append the data from the temporary file back into the modified file. dBASE III will perform steps (1) and (3) for you automatically. *If you are using dBASE II, you must perform all three steps yourself.* Make sure you read the section which pertains to your version of dBASE.

The method of modifying the structure of a dBASE III file is below. The method of modifying a dBASE II file is on the following page.

Modifying the Structure of a dBASE III File

If you are using dBASE II, do not use this section. You will lose all your data! See the following page.

First, use the DISPLAY STRUCTURE command (F5 key) to display the structure as it exists. You may decide to leave things alone.

Changes may be necessary, however. You may have not made a field wide enough, or need more decimal places, or need to change the type of field. If so, give the command MODIFY STRUCTURE. You will be shown a full screen version of the file structure which you can modify using many of the full screen editing commands. (This is similar to the screen you completed in the CREATE command). It is possible to add fields, delete fields, and change the size of fields by simply changing the specification that appears before you.

To insert a field, type ^N (Ctrl-N); to delete a field, type ^U (Ctrl-U). Other structure changes are made by editing the structure displayed. For instance, to change field name, simply type over the old name.

To change field type you have to be very careful. If you change field type, exit MODIFY STRUCTURE and restart before making any other changes.

Do not change both field name and field length (width) at the same time. Change names, exit MODIFY STRUCTURE, then reenter MODIFY STRUCTURE to change the widths.

When the structure is the way you want it to be, exit from MODIFY STRUCTURE by typing ^End (Ctrl-End). dBASE III will automatically retrieve the data which existed in the data file prior to modification. Check the results with the DISPLAY STRUCTURE command. If the effect is not what you want, you may repeat the process.

End of the dBASE III MODIFY STRUCTURE section. dBASE III users ignore the following section.

Modifying the Structure of a dBASE II File

If you are using dBASE III, do not use this section. You will ruin your data file!

First, use the DISPLAY STRUCTURE command to display the structure as it exists. You may decide to leave things alone.

Changes may be necessary, however. You may have not made a field wide enough, or need more decimal places, or need to change the type of field. If you insist on modifying the structure, the first step is to copy the data file to a temporary data file. I always use COPY TO TEMP to keep things simple and obvious.

Once the COPY TO TEMP is finished, issue the command MODIFY STRUCTURE . You will be asked if you really wish to proceed -- answer "y" and the data in the data file is lost forever (except if you copied it to TEMP.DBF as noted above).

Once you answer "y" you will be shown a full screen version of the file structure which you can modify using many of the full screen editing commands. It is possible to add fields, delete fields, and change the size of fields by simply changing the specification that appears before you. Note: To change field type you have to be a bit trickier. Changing the type in this mode may cause you to lose the original data. Before changing field type, sign out the dBASE II manual and read it carefully.

When the structure is the way you want it to be, exit from MODIFY STRUCTURE by typing ^W (Ctrl-W). Check the results with the DISPLAY STRUCTURE command. If all is OK, proceed.

The final step is to retrieve the data written to the temporary file and append it to the file whose structure was modified. In this example, APPEND FROM TEMP would have the following effect: fields in the TEMP file with the same field name and type would be inserted into the (modified) file. If the appended field is shorter than the modified field, then blanks are added. If the appended field is longer, then it will be truncated. If there is no field in the modified file corresponding to a field in the appended file, then the data is discarded. If a field in the modified file is not in the appended file, then the field is filled with blanks.

End of the dBASE II MODIFY STRUCTURE section.

GUIDED ACTIVITY

This activity requires you to use the data file modification commands.

1. Follow the startup procedure for your version of dBASE as outlined in Unit 2.

2. USE RAW2 , the data file which you created in the Guided Activity following Unit 7.

3. Using the REPLACE command, increase all costs by 20%. This operation is illustrated in Figure 8-1.

✔**CHECKPOINT**
What command do you use to increase all costs by 20%?

_____

4. Using the CHANGE command, change the following quantities:

Stock Number	Quantity on Hand
0014	200
0015	229
0013	91

If you are quite clever, you will be able to structure the CHANGE command so that it only presents those three records.

✔**CHECKPOINT**
What command would you use to change only those three records?

_____

5. DELETE all records which have 100 or more units on hand, then LIST the data base. Are all 17 records displayed? SET DELETED ON and LIST again. You should have only two records this time. Give the command that will remove the deleted flags. This operation is illustrated in Figure 8-3.

✔**CHECKPOINT**
What command will perform the deletion?

_____

✔**CHECKPOINT**
What commands do you use to remove the deleted flags?

_____

6. MODIFY STRUCTURE to change the width of the cost field to five columns. Make sure you use the version appropriate for your version of dBASE.

7. When you have completed all of the above, give the command QUIT to exit dBASE. Remember to backup your work. If everything is proper, turn off the computer and return the dBASE software to the Lab Supervisor.

REVIEW QUESTIONS

1. What are the four types of changes that can be made to a data file. Give a reason for performing each.

2. Which command(s) would you use in each of the following situations (use any appropriate field name):

   *a. to increase everybody's age by one year.

   *b. to review and change as necessary the phone numbers of all persons in the Marketing department.

   *c. to change Robert Smith's last name to Smith-Jones.

3. What is the difference between

   a. SET DELETED ON and DELETE

   b. DELETE and PACK

   c. PACK and ZAP

   d. SET DELETED OFF and RECALL

4. Predict what would happen if

   a. you followed the dBASE III procedure to modify the structure of a dBASE II file.

   b. you followed the dBASE II procedure to modify the structure of a dBASE III file.

DOCUMENTATION RESEARCH

Using the reference manual, determine the answer to the following questions which deal with the commands discussed in this Unit. I recommend you also write the page number by the discussion of the command, above.

1. APPEND FROM {filename} -- what will happen if the field width of the file in USE (the target file) is less than the field width of the FROM (source) file?

2. REPLACE {scope} {field} WITH {expression} FOR {condition} -- what happens to the index if the replacement affects a field that is part of the index key?

3. CHANGE FIELDS {field list} FOR {condition} -- how do you edit a memo field?

4. DELETE {scope} FOR {condition} -- if neither {scope} nor {condition} are specified, how many records will be marked for deletion?

5. RECALL {scope} FOR {condition} -- what effect does this command have on records that have been removed by PACK or ZAP commands?

6. PACK -- what effect does this command have on open index files?

7. ZAP -- what effect does SET SAFETY ON have on this command?

Application

C MILWAUKEE BANKS

In this application exercise, you will conduct inquiry and data file modification operations.

1. Start by signing out the dBASE manual and software, as well as the EXERCISES disk.

2. Insert the EXERCISES disk in the Left (A) drive. Insert a formatted disk in the B drive. This disk will hold the files that you create and edit.*

3. Reset or turn on the machine, as appropriate. Remember to enter the date and time as prompted.

4. Once the system is loaded and the date and time set you should see the DOS command prompt (A>_). Give the command

    copy mil_bank.dbf b:

   which will copy a database file from the EXERCISES disk to your disk.

5. Once the copying is finished, remove the EXERCISES disk and follow the startup procedure for your version of dBASE as outlined in Unit 2.

6. For the remainder of this exercise, you will make extensive use of the data file MIL_BANK,** which you have copied onto your data disk. USE the file, and display its structure. Assets, Deposits, Loans, Operating Income, and Operating Expenses fields are in units of 1000, i.e., multiply assets * 1000 to get actual assets. Where a field = 0, the data were not available. Banks which were not ranked in the top 25 in 1983 are given a RANK_83 = 26.

---

* If you are using a fixed disk PC, your instructor will tell you how to do steps 2-4.
** The data in this file are excerpted from a list published by *The Business Journal Serving Greater Milwaukee* in 1984.

```
Record#  RANK_84 NAME                                  ADDRESS
                   TELEPHONE CEO           ASSETS DEPOSITS   LOANS OP_INC
OME OP_EXPENSE RET_ON_ASS HOLDING_CO              HO_CO_TKR DIVIDEND
  RANK_83
      1        1 First Wisconsin National Bank of Milwaukee 777 E. Wisconsin Ave
., Milwaukee          765-4321  Hal Kuehl       3422805 2365040 2428042    296
811     291040        0.320 First Wisconsin Corp.          FWC         1.0875
        1
      2        2 M&I Marshall & Ilsley Bank              770 N. Water St., Mi
lwaukee               765-7700  J. A. Puelicher 1576133  834640  788418    142
131     129094        0.860 Marshall & Ilsley Corp.       MNI         1.9600
        2
      3        3 Marine Bank, N.A.                       111 E. Wisconsin Ave
., Milwaukee          765-3000  George Slater   1446316 1036087  972377    114
461     108410        0.630 Marine Corp.                  MAR         1.1600
        3
      4        4 First Bank Milwaukee                    201 W. Wisconsin Ave
., Milwaukee          278-6000  Jay Walters      725397  571862  420382     52
235      50853        0.260 First Bank System Inc.        FBS         2.8000
        4
      5        5 Heritage Bank                           2323 N. Mayfair Road
, Wauwatosa           771-8100  Richard Jacobus  413913  341436  242780     34
180      31343        0.000 Heritage Wisconsin Corp.      HWC         0.6000
        5
Press any key to continue..._
```

FIGURE C-1 Display of All Fields

7. DISPLAY ALL . You will notice that the records are too wide to fit on one line of the screen (see Figure C-1). With this data file, you will have to use the form DISPLAY ALL {list} to display just the fields you are interested in.

   For instance, to display the names of the banks, give the command

      display all name

   (see Figure C-2).

8. Below are several questions which you must answer using the MIL_BANK data file. There are many ways to answer these questions: you can list the relevant field(s) and count the occurrences or compute the ratio asked for; better, you can list the relevant field(s) for only those records that meet the condition; or, best, when data from individual records are not requested, you can use the summary statistics and not list anything. In some cases, you will have to create a temporary index.

```
. display all name
Record#   name
       1  First Wisconsin National Bank of Milwaukee
       2  M&I Marshall & Ilsley Bank
       3  Marine Bank, N.A.
       4  First Bank Milwaukee
       5  Heritage Bank
       6  Marine Bank West
       7  M&I Northern Bank
       8  Independence Bank Waukesha
       9  Marine First National Bank of Racine
      10  F&M Bank
      11  Waukesha State Bank
      12  Heritage Bank and Trust
      13  M&I Wauwatosa State Bank
      14  Continental Bank & Trust Co.
      15  First Bank Southeast N.A.
      16  Milwaukee County Bank
      17  M&I First National Bank
      18  Park State Bank
      19  M&I Bank of Racine
      20  First Interstate Bank -- West Allis
Press any key to continue..._
```

FIGURE C-2 Display of a Single Field
Note: Item entered by the user is in **boldface**.

As you determine the answers to the questions, make screen prints (i.e., <SHIFT>PrtSc) and circle the answer. Also, identify the screen print by writing the question number (e.g., 8a.) on it.

a. How many banks are affiliated with the Holding Company of Marshall & Ilsley Corp.?

To answer this question, you need to know how to identify banks which are affiliated with a particular holding company, then how to identify those which are affiliated with this particular holding company.

We do another DISPLAY STRUCTURE and notice that there is a field named HOLDING_CO. We give the command

display all name,holding_co

and note that there are several banks that list "Marshall & Ilsley Corp" as the holding company. We could simply count them on our fingers, but we decide to be more elegant.

The next step is display only those banks with the holding company of Marshall & Ilsley Corp. The command which will do this is

    display name,holding_co for holding_co='Marshall & Ilsley'

We do not have to specify the entire match string ('Marshall & Ilsley Corp.'), but what we do specify will be checked starting in byte one of the field and extending as far as the length of the match string. This command will give us a list of only the banks we are interested in, but we still must use our fingers to count them.

Remembering that dBASE has a COUNT command, we next give the command

    count for holding_co='Marshall & Ilsley'

which yields the answer directly.

b. How many banks are in Milwaukee?

Our first inclination is to give the command COUNT FOR CITY='Milwaukee' but that will not work because there is no field named CITY. With a bit of thought, we find a field named ADDRESS, but soon discover that the city is not the first item in ADDRESS. We must therefore write a conditional expression which is true when the string 'Milwaukee' appears in the field ADDRESS. Recalling the substring comparison operator -- $ -- we use the command

    count for 'Milwaukee'$address

which will work reasonably well. For intellectual exercise, try to think of a situation where this command would yield an answer which is greater than the number of banks which are in the city of Milwaukee.

c. How many banks are ranked higher in 1984 than in 1983? A lower number indicates a "higher rank," thus a bank with 1984 ranking of 8 and a 1983 ranking of 9 would rank higher in 1984 than in 1983.

This is another count operation, but this time the conditional expression must be true only when one field is greater than the other. I leave it to you to determine the condition.

d. Which bank(s) had operating expenses higher than operating income?

This is not a count operation. Here you must display the name of the bank(s) for which the condition OP_EXPENSE > OP_INCOME is true.

e. If the banks were ranked by loans instead of assets, which would be ninth largest?

To answer this question, you must create a temporary index based on the field containing loans. Then you must figure out how to determine which bank is ninth largest. I recommend the following commands:

    index on -1*loans to temp
    display next 9 name

The first command builds the index in descending order of loans; the second command lists the top nine, the last in the list being the answer sought.

f. What is the ratio of assets:deposits for Milwaukee County Bank?

There are three things you must determine here. First, what is meant by ratio of assets:deposits; second, how do we get dBASE to calculate that ratio; third, how do we get dBASE to calculate the ratio for a specific bank?

A ratio is the quotient of two numbers. The result is usually expressed as "something to 1," as in 2:1 when the first number is twice the amount of the second. Therefore, the asset:deposit ratio will be the result of dividing the assets by the deposits.

dBASE will calculate and display mathematical results as a part of the DISPLAY command. To print the name and asset:deposit ratio of all records, simply give the command

    display all name,assets/deposits

We can either scan the list for Milwaukee County Bank, or we could further modify the command to be

    display name,assets/deposits for name='Milwaukee County Bank'

g. Which bank has the highest ratio of assets:deposits?

You should be able to do this one by yourself.

9. Copy the file to a new file called NEW_BANK.

10. USE NEW_BANK

11. Use the REPLACE command to change the dividend to 1.46 for all banks affiliated with the Holding Company of Marine Corp.

12. Use the DELETE command to delete all banks with the Holding Company of 'none.' List all bank names on the printer.

13. SET DELETED ON , then list all bank names on the printer again.

14. When you are finished with all of the above, QUIT to exit dBASE. Remember to backup your work, turn off the computer, and return the dBASE software and EXERCISES disk to the Lab Supervisor.

Unit

9 REPORT GENERATION

This unit deals with the creation and production of reports. The exact procedure differs between dBASE III and dBASE II, but the general considerations are the same. This unit will discuss those general considerations and will then provide specific instructions for preparing reports in both versions of dBASE.

LEARNING OBJECTIVES

1. At the completion of this unit you should know the terminology of reports.

2. At the completion of this unit you should be able to create and produce a report.

IMPORTANT COMMANDS

    MODIFY REPORT {form file}
    REPORT FORM {form file}

GENERAL CONSIDERATIONS

A report is a method of displaying the data in a data file. There are three parts to a report: the heading, the body of the report, and totals and subtotals. Not all reports will be composed of all three parts. The report heading contains identifying information, such as page number, date, and title. The report body includes column headings and can include data from individual records, or it may contain only summary data. The report may also contain totals and sub-totals of numeric data, and may be grouped according to some key. The data included in the body of the report may be arranged in a specific order, and may be all data in the file or a subset of the data file.

Page No.   1
10/20/85
                        Raw Materials Inventory Report

                        prepared by Steven C. Ross

ID	Description	Cost per Unit	Quantity on Hand	Material Value	Last Order Date	Inventory Age (days)
0014	12 oz. cup	0.03	300	9.00	10/04/85	16
0015	16 oz. cup	0.05	400	20.00	09/28/85	22
0018	4 oz. fry pack	0.02	332	6.64	10/19/85	1
0019	6 oz. fry pack	0.03	500	15.00	10/15/85	5
0013	8 oz. cup	0.02	600	12.00	10/06/85	14
0011	Coca Cola (oz.)	0.05	800	40.00	10/13/85	7
0012	Sprite (oz.)	0.05	700	35.00	10/12/85	8
0001	all-beef patty	0.10	100	10.00	10/01/85	19
0016	apple pie	0.16	346	55.36	08/15/85	66
0009	catsup (oz.)	0.04	386	15.44	10/10/85	10
0006	ch. onion (oz.)	0.06	876	52.56	10/10/85	10
0004	cheese slice	0.02	255	5.10	10/09/85	11
0017	cherry pie	0.14	200	28.00	09/19/85	31
0010	fren. fry (oz.)	0.01	999	9.99	10/12/85	8
0003	lettuce leaf	0.01	90	0.90	10/03/85	17
0005	pickle slice	0.03	900	27.00	09/15/85	35
0008	regular bun	0.10	200	20.00	10/03/85	17
0007	sesame seed bun	0.12	400	48.00	10/08/85	12
0002	sp. sauce (oz.)	0.01	400	4.00	09/30/85	20

*** Total ***

                                        413.99

FIGURE 9-1 Sample dBASE III Report

The general operation of a report generator is that it first prints the heading and column headings, then scans each record of the report in physical or logical order (the latter if the file is opened with an index). If the record is to be included in the report, the contents of the record are formatted according to the report format and printed on screen or paper. Totals and sub-totals are accumulated and printed as appropriate.

The body of the report is defined by the report format. This includes information on column contents, column width, decimal places for numeric data, whether or not numeric data in the column is to be totaled (and sub-totaled), and the column heading. In dBASE, the term report field (or field) is used to mean report column. It may be useful to think of the report format as a template for the output of the data.

```
=====================================================================
|  CURSOR   <-- -->   |        UP   DOWN  |    DELETE     | Insert Mode:  Ins  |
|   Char:     ←  →    | Field:  ↑     ↓   | Char:  Del    | Exit:        ^End  |
|   Word:  Home End   | Page:  PgUp PgDn  | Field: ^Y     | Abort:        Esc  |
|   Pan:     ^← ^→    | Help:   Fl        | Column: ^U    | Jump:        ^Home |
=====================================================================

                         Page heading:




                Page width (# chars):        80
                Left margin (# chars):        8
                Right margin (# chars):       0
                # lines/page:                58
                Double space report? (Y/N):   N
```

FIGURE 9-2 Blank Report Heading Page
Note: Editing information displayed at top of screen

A sample report is contained in Figure 9-1. The heading area contains page number, date, and title information. The body of the report contains information drawn from the RAW_MATL data file, including some calculated fields (columns). Notice that one field is totaled, with the result at the end of the report.

The remainder of this unit is devoted to a discussion of the creation and preparation of the sample report.

CREATING THE REPORT FORMAT IN dBASE III

In dBASE III, the report format is created or edited with one command and executed with another. The format is stored in a disk file with a .FRM extension. In this section we discuss how to create and modify a report format.

dBASE III provides two commands to create and modify report format files. Either

CREATE REPORT {form file}

or

MODIFY REPORT {form file}

```
Structure of file B:raw_matl.dbf
========================================================================
RMID        C    4   | LAST_ORDER D   8   |                |
DESC        C   15   |                    |                |
COST        N    8  2|                    |                |
INVENTORY   N    3   |                    |                |
========================================================================
                         Page heading:


   Raw Materials Inventory Report

   prepared by Steven C. Ross




               Page width (# chars):         80
               Left margin (# chars):         8
               Right margin (# chars):        0
               # lines/page:                 58
               Double space report?  (Y/N):   N
```

FIGURE 9-3 Completed Report Heading Page
Note: Items entered by the user are in **boldface**

is used to create or modify a report format file for use with the report command (below). Example:

    modify report raw__matl

You will be led through a series of screens as the form file is created or modified. The form file will have the extension .FRM . Before starting the report creation process, USE the file from which the data will be reported.

   The first screen allows you to enter a heading of up to four lines and to specify parameters such as page width, left and right margins, number of lines per page, and the spacing of the report. Whatever is entered in the heading section will be centered on the page when the report is printed. The top of the screen will either show cursor movement commands and other editing information or the structure of the data file. Toggle between the two with the F1 key. (All the examples in this unit except Figure 9-2 show the structure alternative).

```
Structure of file B:raw_matl.dbf
==================================================================================
RMID        C    4   LAST_ORDER D   8   |                      |
DESC        C   15                      |                      |
COST        N    8  2                   |                      |
INVENTORY   N    3                      |                      |
==================================================================================
Group/subtotal on:




Summary report only? (Y/N): N          Eject after each group/subtotal? (Y/N): N

Group/subtotal heading:



Subgroup/sub-subtotal on:




Subgroup/subsubtotal heading:
```

FIGURE 9-4   Blank Group/Subtotal Screen

When the MODIFY REPORT command is first given, the screen clears and the first page of the report format appears, as illustrated in Figure 9-2. Figure 9-3 illustrates the first page with a heading entered. Although none of the format parameters were changed in this example, you can change page width, etc., by making appropriate entries on this page.

The second screen allows you to specify a key field upon which group subtotals will be computed. If your file is sorted or indexed on a field, and you want a subtotal for each different value of the field, then make appropriate entries here. If you do not want group subtotals, skip this screen by typing the PgDn key. The group/subtotal screen is illustrated in Figure 9-4.

If you use a subtotals field, the file should be indexed or sorted on that field. The report will start a new subtotal each time the subtotals field changes, and an unindexed/unsorted file will not produce the report you intended.

On the third and subsequent screens, you define each column ("field") of the report. A blank field definition screen appears as Figure 9-5. First, the field contents is specified. The field contents may be a database field, a memory variable, a character

```
Structure of file B:raw_matl.dbf
==================================================================
RMID         C    4  | LAST_ORDER D   8  |                    |
DESC         C   15   |                  |                    |
COST         N    8  2|                  |                    |
INVENTORY    N    3   |                  |                    |
==================================================================
                                   Field  1        Columns left =    72
>>>>>>>>---------------------------------------------------------------



 Field
   contents


                                 # decimal places:  0  Total? (Y/N): N


            1
 Field      2
   header    3
            4
 Width       1
```

FIGURE 9-5 Blank Field Definition Screen

string, or a computed result.

To help you specify field contents, you may press the F1 key which will display the structure of the file in USE at the top of the screen. If the field contents is a numeric value, then you will be asked to specify the number of decimal places and whether or not you wish to total that field.

Once the contents of the field is defined, you may specify a field (i.e., column) header of up to four lines. Finally, the field width is specified. The width will default to the wider of the heading or the field, but you may enter a different width if you wish.

Completed field definition screens are illustrated in Figures 9-6 and 9-7. The field in the first figure is fairly simple. It is based on one data file field (RMID), and is a character type field so no decimal places or totals need be specified. The field in the second figure is more complex. It is the numeric product of two fields (COST and INVENTORY), will be totaled, with two decimal places.

```
Structure of file B:raw_matl.dbf
========================================================================
RMID        C    4  |LAST_ORDER D   8  |              |
DESC        C   15     |                |              |
COST        N    8  2  |                |              |
INVENTORY   N    3     |                |              |
========================================================================
                                    Field  1          Columns left =   72
>>>>>>>>-------------------------------------------------------------------



Field        rmid
   contents



                                    # decimal places:  0  Total? (Y/N): N

             1 ID
Field        2
   header    3
             4
Width        4
```

FIGURE 9-6 Completed Field Definition Screen
Note: Items entered by the user are in **boldface**

dBASE functions may also be included in field definitions. For example, the last field in this report (Inventory Age) is computed by subtracting the date of last order from the system date: DATE( )-LAST_ORDER .

As you create or modify your report, the screen will display an illustration of the headings and field formats, as well as an indication of the number of columns remaining. This information will appear on the screen between the file structure and the field contents.

You may move among the screens with the PgUp and PgDn keys.

When finished, type ^End (Ctrl-End) to exit.

To make changes later, give the MODIFY REPORT command and you may move through the screens making changes as desired.

```
Structure of file B:raw_matl.dbf
==========================================================================
RMID        C   4   LAST_ORDER D   8
DESC        C  15
COST        N   8  2
INVENTORY   N   3
==========================================================================
                              Field  5              Columns left =   20
>>>>>>>>ID   Description   Cost   Quantity Material  --------------------
                          per    on Hand  Value
                          Unit


        XXXX XXXXXXXXXXXXXXX 99999.99      999 #########.##

Field            cost*inventory
   contents


                                      # decimal places:  2  Total? (Y/N): Y


                1Material
Field           2Value
   header        3
                 4
Width            12
```

FIGURE 9-7 Completed Field Definition Screen
Note: Items entered by the user are in **boldface**

PRODUCING THE REPORT IN dBASE III

Once the report format is created or modified, the REPORT FORM command is used to
produce the report. The general form of the command is

REPORT FORM {form file}

which will produce the report on the screen. dBASE assumes that the {form file} has
a .FRM extension.

dBASE will output the report in the same order the data appears in the data file. If
you want a special order, or if you are using groups and subtotals, sort or index the file
before giving the REPORT FORM command.

Alternate versions of the command may be used:

REPORT FORM {form file} TO PRINT
REPORT FORM {form file} TO PRINT NOEJECT

REPORT FORM {form file} FOR {condition}
REPORT FORM {form file} TO FILE {file name}

The effect of the first of these is to send the report to the printer. dBASE gives a page eject before it starts printing the report, unless you specify NOEJECT (second example). The default ("eject") insures that the report always starts on a new page, while the alternate ("no eject") may save paper. To produce the report which appears as Figure 9-1, you will give the command

report form raw_matl to print

Unless you specify a FOR {condition}, dBASE will include all records in the data file in the report. Logical conditions in report commands work just like they do everywhere else in dBASE.

Finally, the report may be sent to a file for inclusion in other documents via a word processor, or perhaps for importation into a spreadsheet. For instance, the report which appears as Figure 9-1 was produced with the command

report form raw_matl to file raw_matl

which created a file named RAW_MATL.TXT which was read into the text for this unit.

REPORT GENERATION IN dBASE II

If you have read the preceding sections, you know that report generation in dBASE III is a two-step process. In dBASE II, both steps are combined. When the REPORT FORM command is given, dBASE will check the default disk drive to see whether or not the form file exists. If not, the file is created based on the answers to several questions. The general form of the command is

REPORT FORM {form file}

If {form file} does not exist, it will be created based on the answers given to several questions -- if it does exist, then the report will be prepared without further ado.

The {form file} consists of a series of answers to questions asked the first time the report is generated. These answers are stored in a file with extension .FRM which may be edited using MODIFY COMMAND {form file}.FRM or any other editor. (The MODIFY COMMAND command is discussed in Unit 12.) The questions asked are illustrated in Figure 9-8.

Note that an expression can be part of the report (column 005). Also note the various means for formatting column headings: < left justifies, > right justifies, and ; is used to split the heading into a second line.

If you use a subtotals field, the file should be indexed or sorted on that field. The report will start a new subtotal each time the subtotals field changes, and an unindexed/unsorted file will not produce the report you intended.

```
ENTER OPTIONS, M=LEFT MARGIN, L=LINES/PAGE, W=PAGE WIDTH M=8
PAGE HEADING? (Y/N) Y
ENTER PAGE HEADING: Raw Materials Inventory Report
DOUBLE SPACE REPORT? (Y/N) N
ARE TOTALS REQUIRED? (Y/N) Y
SUBTOTALS IN REPORT? (Y/N) N
SUMMARY REPORT ONLY? (Y/N) N
EJECT PAGE AFTER SUBTOTALS? (Y/N) N
COL      WIDTH,CONTENTS
001      4,RMID
ENTER HEADING: <ID
002      15,DESC
ENTER HEADING: <Description
003      8,COST
ENTER HEADING: >Cost per;Unit
ARE TOTALS REQUIRED? (Y/N) N
004      9,INVENTORY
ENTER HEADING: >Quantity;on Hand
ARE TOTALS REQUIRED? (Y/N) N
005      12,COST*INVENTORY
ENTER HEADING: >Material;Value
ARE TOTALS REQUIRED? (Y/N) Y
006      8,LAST:ORDER
ENTER HEADING: >Last;Order
007      <CR>
```

FIGURE 9-8 Creating a Report Form in dBASE II
Note: Items entered by the user are in **boldface**

Alternate versions of the command may be used:

REPORT FORM {form file} TO PRINT
REPORT FORM {form file} FOR {condition}

The effect of the first of these is to send the report to the printer. dBASE gives a page eject before it starts printing the report, unless you have previously given a SET EJECT OFF command. This insures that the report always starts on a new page.

Unless you specify a FOR {condition}, dBASE will include all records in the datafile in the report. Conditional expressions in report commands work just like they do everywhere else in dBASE.

```
Structure of file B:raw_matl.dbf
=================================================================
RMID       C    4   |LAST_ORDER D    8  |              |
DESC       C   15                       |              |
COST       N    8  2|                   |              |
INVENTORY  N    3   |                   |              |
=================================================================
                             Field  8              Columns left =    0
tion      Cost      Quantity Material   Last   Inventory
          per       on Hand  Value      Order  Age
          Unit                          Date   (days)

XXXXXXXX 99999.99        999 ########.## xx/xx/xx 9999999999

Field
  contents


                                       # decimal places:  0  Total? (Y/N): N

          1
Field     2
  header  3
          4
Width       1
```

FIGURE 9-9 Field Definition Screen

GUIDED ACTIVITY

This activity requires you to use the report generation commands.

1. Follow the startup procedure for your version of dBASE as outlined in Unit 2.

2. USE RAW_MATL

3. Following the examples provided in this Unit, MODIFY REPORT RAW_MATL (dBASE III) or REPORT FORM RAW_MATL (dBASE II).

4a. If you are using dBASE III, the screen should look like Figure 9-9 after you have defined the last field. Press <CR> before you type anything else in Field 8 and the creation process will be exited. Type REPORT FORM RAW_MATL to produce the report on the screen.

4b. If you are using dBASE II, the screen should look like Figure 9-8 after you have defined the last field. Press <CR> before you type anything else in Field 7 and the creation process will be exited, and the report will be produced on the screen.

5a. If the report on the screen is not correct, and you are using dBASE III, give the command MODIFY REPORT RAW_MATL and correct as necessary. Repeat steps 3 to 5 until your report looks like Figure 9-1 (except that the numbers in the last column will differ because the system date you enter will be different that the date in the example).

5b. If the report on the screen is not correct, and you are using dBASE II, give the command DELETE FILE RAW_MATL.FRM followed by REPORT FORM RAW_MATL and re-enter the report. Repeat steps 3 to 5 until your report looks like Figure 9-1 (except that you will not have the last column because dBASE II does not support date fields).

6. If the report is correct on the screen, give the command REPORT FORM RAW_MATL TO PRINT to print a copy.

7. Print the report in RMID order (hint, you will need an index file).

✔CHECKPOINT
What commands do you use to print this report?

_____

8. When you have completed all of the above, give the command QUIT to exit dBASE. Remember to backup your work. If everything is proper, turn off the computer and return the dBASE software to the Lab Supervisor.

REVIEW QUESTIONS

1. Define the following terms:

   a. report

   b. report heading

   c. report body

   d. totals

   e. report field

*2. Assume that you have created RAW_MATL.FRM. What sequence of commands would you give to print the report in RMID order?

DOCUMENTATION RESEARCH

Using the reference manual, determine the answer to the following questions which deal with the commands discussed in this Unit. I recommend you also write the page number by the discussion of the command, above.

1. MODIFY REPORT {form file} -- what is the options menu, and how is it accessed?

2. REPORT FORM {form file} -- what is the effect of the PLAIN and HEADING options?

10 LABEL GENERATION

This unit deals with the creation and production of labels. The label commands are available only in dBASE III, so dBASE II users can pass on this unit. The illustrations in this unit deal with the creation of labels for Chez Jacques' inventory, an activity which you will perform at the end of the unit. There is no review section in this Unit.

LEARNING OBJECTIVE

At the completion of this unit you should be able to create labels using dBASE III.

IMPORTANT COMMANDS

MODIFY LABEL {form file}
LABEL FORM {form file}

GENERAL CONSIDERATIONS

Labels are very much like reports, in that they are a method of displaying the data in a data file. The label commands in dBASE III are provided so you may create output in a form suitable for use as mailing or package labels. See Figure 10-1 for sample labels.

Data displayed in labels may be data file fields, character strings, or memory variables. All label entries must be character type data, which means that you must convert numeric and date type data to character type before inclusion in a label.

Similar to the report commands, label creation is a two step process. First, a label format file is created. Then, the labels are printed based on some or all of the data file data.

```
Chez Jacques Inventory          Chez Jacques Inventory
RMID: 0014                      RMID: 0015
12 oz. cup                      16 oz. cup
Cost:     0.03                  Cost:     0.05
Last Ordered: 10/04/85          Last Ordered: 09/28/85


Chez Jacques Inventory          Chez Jacques Inventory
RMID: 0018                      RMID: 0019
4 oz. fry pack                  6 oz. fry pack
Cost:     0.02                  Cost:     0.03
Last Ordered: 10/19/85          Last Ordered: 10/15/85


Chez Jacques Inventory
RMID: 0002
sp. sauce (oz.)
Cost:     0.01
Last Ordered: 09/30/85
```

FIGURE 10-1 Sample Labels
Note: partial set, not all labels displayed

Before creating the label, you should acquire the medium on which the labels will be printed. This is usually a special computer form consisting of self-adhesive labels on a perforated backing sheet with pin feed holes along the edge. Depending on the size of the printer, this form may vary in width up to 15 inches wide, with one to four labels across.

Measure the individual label. A typical size is 3 7/16 inch wide by 15/16 inch high. The typical printer prints 10 characters per inch (wide) and 6 lines per inch (high), which means that five 34-character lines will fit on this label. Fortunately for us, that is the default label size for dBASE III. If your label or printer are different, you may have to change the default values on the label dimensions screen.

For practice and testing, you may use regular computer paper. The most common paper is 8 1/2 inches wide and 11 inches long, which will support 22 labels (2 wide x 11 deep).

The ranges of label specifications are

width of label	1 - 120 characters
height of label	1 - 16 lines
left margin	0 - 250
lines between labels	0 - 16 (vertical)
spaces between labels	0 - 120 (horizontal)
number of labels across	1 - 52
width of all labels on line	1 - 250 characters

```
Structure of file B:raw_matl.dbf
=================================================================================
RMID         C    4    LAST_ORDER D    8
DESC         C   15
COST         N    8   2
INVENTORY    N    3
=================================================================================

                    Width of label:            35
                    Height of label:            5
                    Left margin:                0
                    Lines between labels:       1
                    Spaces between labels:      0
                    Number of labels across:    1

Remarks:
```

FIGURE 10-2 Blank Label Dimensions Screen

CREATING THE LABEL FORMAT

The label format is stored in a file with a .LBL extension. Two commands are provided to create or modify the label format file, either

    CREATE LABEL {form file}
or
    MODIFY LABEL {form file}

is used to create or modify a label format file for use with the LABEL command (below). Example:

    modify label raw_matl

Before issuing the command, open (USE) the data file from which the labels will be produced.

There are two screens for the creation or modification of the label format. The first screen (Figures 10-2 and 10-3) is provided for dimensional information, while the second screen (Figures 10-4 and 10-5) is provided for label contents.

Completing the dimensional screen is usually quite easy. In the example case, the "Number of labels across: " entry was changed to 2, and the name of the person and the date were entered in the "Remarks: " line. (Compare Figures 10-2 and 10-3.) Default values were acceptable for everything else.

```
Structure of file B:raw_matl.dbf
==================================================================
RMID         C   4    LAST_ORDER D   8
DESC         C  15
COST         N   8  2
INVENTORY    N   3
==================================================================

                Width of label:          35
                Height of label:          5
                Left margin:              0
                Lines between labels:     1
                Spaces between labels:    0
                Number of labels across:  2

Remarks:   Steven C. Ross, 6/26/85
```

FIGURE 10-3 Completed Label Dimensions Screen
Note: Items entered by the user are in **boldface**

The label contents screen is more of a challenge. Labels may not contain numeric or date type data, so any information from fields of those types must be converted to character type data. We will discuss each line of the label contents -- refer to Figure 10-1 for the finished product and Figure 10-5 for the label structure.

The first line of the label is composed of the text 'Chez Jacques Inventory'. This is a character string which will be constant on each label. Note that such character strings are enclosed in quotation marks.

The second line of the label is a combination of the character string 'RMID: ' and the field RMID, joined by the + (string concatenation) operator.

The third line consists of the field DESC.

The fourth line is the combination of the string 'Cost: ' and the expression STR(COST,8,2). Recall from Unit 4 that the STR(numeric expression,length,decimals) (string function) evaluates a numeric expression and yields a character string. In this instance, the numeric expression is the COST field, and the length and decimals were set to be the same as the field (8 and 2).

The fifth line consists of the string 'Last Ordered: ' and the character equivalent of the field LAST_ORDER -- DTOC(LAST_ORDER). The DTOC(date expression) (date to character function) is used to convert the date type field to character type data for the label.

```
Structure of file B:raw_matl.dbf
========================================================================
RMID       C   4  │LAST_ORDER D   8  │              │              │
DESC       C  15  │                  │              │              │
COST       N   8  2                  │              │              │
INVENTORY  N   3  │                  │              │              │
========================================================================

                                 Label contents:
           1
           2
           3
           4
           5
```

FIGURE 10-4 Blank Label Contents Screen

PRODUCING THE LABELS

Once the label format is created or modified, the LABEL FORM command is used to produce the labels. The general form of the command is

    LABEL FORM {form file}

which will produce the labels on the screen. dBASE assumes that the {form file} has a .LBL extension.

dBASE will output the labels in the same order the data appears in the data file. If you want a special order, sort or index the file before giving the LABEL FORM command.

Alternate versions of the command may be used:

    LABEL FORM {form file} SAMPLE
    LABEL FORM {form file} TO PRINT
    LABEL FORM {form file} FOR {condition}
    LABEL FORM {form file} TO FILE {file name}

The effect of the first of these is to print test labels to assure proper alignment of the forms in the printer.

The second version will send the labels to the printer. To produce the labels which appears as Figure 10-1, you will give the command

    label form raw_matl to print

```
Structure of file B:raw_matl.dbf              INSERT
=======================================================================
RMID       C    4  | LAST_ORDER D   8  |                 |
DESC       C   15  |                   |                 |
COST       N    8  2                   |                 |
INVENTORY  N    3  |                   |                 |
=======================================================================

                           Label contents:
        1 'Chez Jacques Inventory'
        2 'RMID: '+rmid
        3 desc
        4 'Cost: '+str(cost,8,2)
        5 'Last Ordered: '+dtoc(last_order)
```

FIGURE 10-5 Completed Label Contents Screen
Note: Items entered by the user are in **boldface**

Unless you specify a FOR {condition}, dBASE will include all records in the data file in the labels. Conditional expressions in label commands work just like they do everywhere else in dBASE.

Finally, the labels may be sent to a file for inclusion in other documents via a word processor, or perhaps for importation into a spreadsheet. For instance, the labels which appear as Figure 10-1 were produced with the command

    label form raw_matl to file raw_labl

which created a file named RAW_LABL.TXT which was read into the text for this unit.

GUIDED ACTIVITY

This activity requires you to use the label generation commands.

1. Follow the startup procedure for your version of dBASE as outlined in Unit 2.

2. USE RAW_MATL

3. Following the examples provided in this Unit, MODIFY LABEL RAW_MATL

4. The the screen should look like Figure 10-5 after you have defined the contents. Type Ctrl-End to exit the creation process. Type LABEL FORM RAW_MATL to produce the labels on the screen.

5. If the labels on the screen are not correct, give the command MODIFY LABEL

RAW_MATL and correct as necessary. Repeat steps 3 and 4 until your labels look like Figure 10-1 (except that you will have more labels than shown in that figure).

6. If the labels are correct on the screen, give the command LABEL FORM RAW_MATL TO PRINT to print a copy.

7. Print the labels in RMID order (hint, you will need an index file).

✔CHECKPOINT

What commands do you use to print the labels in RMID order?

_____

8. When you have completed all of the above, give the command QUIT to exit dBASE. Remember to backup your work. If everything is proper, turn off the computer and return the dBASE software to the Lab Supervisor.

DOCUMENTATION RESEARCH

Using the reference manual, determine the answer to the following questions which deal with the commands discussed in this Unit. I recommend you also write the page number by the discussion of the command, above.

1. MODIFY LABEL {form file} -- how do you reach a submenu of standard label types?

2. MODIFY LABEL {form file} -- how can you remove excess blanks from a label line?

3. LABEL FORM {form file} -- how does the SAMPLE option function?

Application

D ED & BRUCE
SPECIALTIES (I)

This application exercise requires you to use the reporting and label commands in a data file.

1. Start by signing out the dBASE manual and software, as well as the EXERCISES disk.

2. Insert the EXERCISES Disk in the Left (A) drive, and your data disk in the B drive.*

3. Reset or turn on the machine, as appropriate. Remember to enter the date and time as prompted.

4. Once the system is loaded and the date and time set, give the command

    copy mailing.dbf b:

   which will copy a database file from the EXERCISES disk to your disk.

5. Once the copying is finished, remove the system disk and follow the startup procedure for your version of dBASE as outlined in Unit 2.

6. Ed and Bruce Specialties (E&BS) is a small mail-order company which specializes in clothes, gadgets, and specialty foods. One of the data files kept by E&BS is a list of customer names, addresses, and whether or not that customer has ordered each of the three types of merchandise. This is the MAILING.DBF file.

---

* If you are using a fixed disk PC, your instructor will tell you how to accomplish steps 2-4.

The structure of the file is

Field	Field name	Type	Width	Dec
1	LAST_NAME	Character	15	
2	FIRST_NAME	Character	10	
3	STREET	Character	26	
4	CITY	Character	14	
5	STATE	Character	2	
6	ZIP	Character	5	
7	CLOTHES	Logical	1	
8	GADGETS	Logical	1	
9	SP_FOOD	Logical	1	

Fields 1-6 are self-explanatory. Fields 7-9 are True if the customer has ordered that particular type of merchandise within the last three years, and False otherwise. If, for instance, you wished to obtain a list of all persons who had ordered clothes, the command would be LIST FOR CLOTHES . These may be combined with the logical operators, e.g., LIST FOR .NOT. CLOTHES produces a list of those who have not ordered clothes. Other examples are below.

7. You have been asked to query the file and provide certain outputs:

    a. A list containing the names and cities of those who have purchased items in all of the three categories.

    b. A set of mailing labels for those who have ordered tools, but have not ordered clothes. (dBASE III only)

    c. A report showing names and states of those who have not ordered from any of the categories.

    Each of these outputs requires that you develop a logical condition. For the labels and report, you must also create format files. Name the format files EBS.FRM and EBS.LBL . (Remember that dBASE will automatically add the extensions .FRM and .LBL .) The following commands may give you some hints (but they are not the exact commands necessary to accomplish the above).

    ```
    list off city,state,zip for clothes .and. gadgets
    label form ebs for sp_food .and. (.not. gadgets)
    report form ebs for .not. clothes
    ```

8. When you are finished with the above, QUIT to exit dBASE. Remember to backup your work, turn off the computer, and return the dBASE software and EXERCISES disk to the Lab Supervisor.

Part

3

ADVANCED DATA BASE OPERATIONS

In this part we will discuss advanced data base operations. These include the use of command files to automate data base operations as well as the use of multiple data files at once.

The first three units in this part address the creation and use of memory variables and command files. Command files are an extremely important part of the dBASE system because they allow you to save and repeat a series of often-used or lengthy commands. Through the use of command files, it is possible to automate much of what is done in dBASE, and to establish a system for use by those with less dBASE facility than yourself. Command files are written in dBASE's own "language" using the commands we discussed previously as well as some others.

The purpose of these units is to provide familiarity with the essentials of dBASE programming. Those who have never written programs will probably need additional instruction before writing complex dBASE programs. These units are designed to provide a basis for the writing of simple but useful programs.

The remainder of the units discuss the use of more than one file at a time, establishing a link between two files, updating one file based on the information contained in another, and creating a new file based on information contained in two others.

The tools discussed in this part allow for the creation of very sophisticated applications. For instance, we will discuss how to link two files together to minimize the duplication of information, and how to use one file to update another. The treatment of these topics will be necessarily brief, but sufficient to expose you to the advanced capabilities of dBASE.

Unit
11
MEMORY VARIABLES

This unit deals with the creation and use of memory variables. Although dBASE is a field- and record-oriented system, there are occasions when it is expedient or necessary to use memory variables for storage of intermediate results. These variables are usually discarded at the end of a program, but they may be written to a disk file for later recovery and use.

Memory variables can be used in the direct mode of operation (i.e., from the dot prompt) or within command files (see the remainder of Part Four).

LEARNING OBJECTIVES

1. At the completion of this unit you should know

    a. the difference between a variable and a field,

    b. the types of memory variables,

    c. how to create and name memory variables.

2. At the completion of this unit you should be able to

    a. create memory variables,

    b. use memory variables in expressions,

    c. determine currently active memory variables,

    d. store memory variables in a disk file,

    e. retrieve memory variables from a disk file,

f. remove memory variables from memory.

IMPORTANT COMMANDS

```
STORE {expression} TO {memory variable}
{memory variable} = {expression}
SAVE TO {filename}
RESTORE FROM {filename}
DISPLAY MEMORY
RELEASE
```


CREATING MEMORY VARIABLES

Most of us who have programmed in a language such as FORTRAN or BASIC have used memory variables as a matter of course. The BASIC statement LET A=5 creates a memory variable called *A*, while LET C=A+B adds the value of variables *A* and *B* and stores the result in *C*. We have become familiar with the idea that a memory variable name represents an address at which something (number or text string) is stored. A given memory variable name represents one piece of data, and we can answer the question "What is the value of A?" (a variable): "The value of A is 5."

In dBASE, we have been using fields as the point of data storage. But a field name is not sufficient to locate a piece of data, we must also know the record number. For instance, referring to the RAW_MATL data file, we we can not answer the question "What is the value of COST?" (a field) until we have the answer to the question "What item are we discussing?" (a record). If asked "What is the cost of an all-beef patty?" then we may answer: "The cost of an all-beef patty is ten cents."

This field and record approach is very useful when we want to store similar information about a number of items. It is less useful when we want to store a unique piece of information, such as the average of the item costs. For such instances, dBASE provides us with memory variables which are used very much like memory variables in BASIC.

Memory variables are created as a result of dBASE commands. Before creating variables, it is useful to understand what the various types of memory variables are and how they may be named.

Types of Memory Variables

Memory variable data types parallel the types of fields. In dBASE III, there are four available types: Character, Date, Numeric, and Logical.*

The type of a memory variable is determined by the method by which it is created. If character or text data is stored in the variable, then it will be a character type variable, and so forth with numeric and logical data.

---

* In dBASE II, the types are Character, Numeric, and Logical.

In dBASE III, date variables are created when date data are stored in the variable. The result of a date plus or minus a date will be a numeric variable, but a date plus or minus a number is another date. This makes sense:

07/24/85 - 07/14/85 = 10

01/14/86 + 5 = 01/19/86

In dBASE III, a subsequent operation may change the type of the variable.*

Memory Variable Names

Memory variable names follow the same rules as field names. The name must start with a letter, and can be up to ten characters long. Acceptable characters are letters (A-Z), numbers (0-9), and the underscore (_) in dBASE III.** There is no difference between upper and lower case.

Each memory variable will have a unique name. Unlike BASIC and some other languages, the name of the variable does not denote data type. Memory variables may have the same names as fields, but you will probably confuse yourself.

I start memory variable names with M_ to differentiate them from data file fields: e.g., M_NAME as a memory variable which corresponds to NAME as a field in my data file.*** If you do create a memory variable with the same name as a field, then you may later refer to that variable by preceding the name with M->, e.g., M->NAME . The "arrow" is a combination of the minus sign and the greater than sign.

The following are legitimate memory variable names:

sum
count2
r2d2
dbase_iii   *dBASE III only*

The name of a given memory variable is assigned when the variable is created with one of the commands discussed below.

Commands which Create Memory Variables

Memory variables are created by the following commands: ACCEPT, COUNT, PARAMETERS, SUM, AVERAGE, INPUT, STORE, and WAIT.

---

* In dBASE II, you should change the name when you change the type.
** In dBASE II, the colon (:) may be used in memory variable names.
*** In dBASE II, I use M: and M:NAME.

The STORE Command is the fundamental variable-creating command. It is the equivalent of a LET statement in BASIC. The general form is

STORE {expression} TO {memory variable}

which computes the value of {expression} if necessary, and stores result in {memory variable}. The variable will be created if it did not already exist.

Examples:

store 'West Virginia' to state
store 200000 to income
store income*.85 to taxes
store income-taxes to net_inc   *dBASE III only*

In dBASE III, you may use the alternate version:

{memory variable} = {expression}

e.g., STATE='West Virginia' .

The AVERAGE, COUNT, and SUM Commands were introduced in Part Two. The result(s) of the commands may be stored in memory variable(s) using the form

AVERAGE {expression list} TO {memory variable list}
COUNT TO {memory variable}
SUM {expression list} TO {memory variable list}

See the earlier discussion for more detail about these commands. Examples (using RAW_MATL data file):

average cost,inventory,cost*inventory to avgcost,avginven,avgvalue
count for cost*inventory>10 to highvalue
sum cost,inventory,cost*inventory to sumcost,suminven,sumvalue

The ACCEPT, INPUT, and WAIT Commands will be discussed in a later unit.

The PARAMETERS Command is used in advanced programming which is beyond the scope of this book.

MANAGING MEMORY VARIABLES

Memory variables are created for temporary use by dBASE, but may be saved in a disk file for later reference. This section discusses housekeeping -- knowing what variables are in use, keeping the computer free of extraneous variables, and moving variables to and from disk storage.

In Memory

Memory variables normally reside in the memory of the computer. Because there are limits to how many variables can be used and how much room is available, the programmer must be aware of what variables are currently in use and how to remove those which are no longer needed.

The DISPLAY MEMORY command displays name, type, and contents of all currently active memory variables, as well as bytes of memory used by the variables. Useful in debugging. This command is among those illustrated in Figure 11-1. The DISPLAY MEMORY command may be given by pressing the F7 key.

The RELEASE command is used to delete all -- RELEASE ALL -- or selected -- RELEASE {list} -- memory variables so that the space may be reused for other memory variables. dBASE II programmers will become quite familiar with this command as they develop more sophisticated applications. It is seldom needed in dBASE III because of better memory management techniques built into that version.

On Disks

There may be occasions when you wish to save the current values of memory variables to a disk file for later use. The command

SAVE TO {filename}

saves all currently defined memory variables to {filename}.MEM (the extension is added automatically by dBASE). You may direct the command to save only a portion of the variables.

To retrieve the variables, use the command

RESTORE FROM {filename}
RESTORE FROM {filename} ADDITIVE

which will restore saved memory variables from {filename}.MEM. The first version will erase all currently active memory variables, the second version will add the restored variables to those already present, as capacity permits.

Examples:

save to memfile
restore from memfile
restore from memfile additive

```
. use raw_matl index raw_matl
. display
Record#   RMID DESC                   COST INVENTORY LAST_ORDER
      8   0001 all-beef patty         0.10       100 10/01/85
. ? cost
   0.10
. cost=cost*2
      0.20
. ? cost
   0.10
. ? m->cost
       0.20
. display memory
COST         pub   N          0.20  (          0.20000000)
    1 variables defined,         9 bytes used
  255 variables available,    5991 bytes available

.
. display
Record#   RMID DESC                   COST INVENTORY LAST_ORDER
      8   0001 all-beef patty         0.10       100 10/01/85
. m_cost=cost*2
      0.20
. ? cost
   0.10
. ? m->cost
       0.20
. ? m_cost
       0.20
. display memory
COST         pub   N          0.20  (          0.20000000)
M_COST       pub   N          0.20  (          0.20000000)
    2 variables defined,        18 bytes used
  254 variables available,    5982 bytes available

. _
```

FIGURE 11-1 Memory Variable Illustration
Note: Commands entered by the user are in **boldface**

USING MEMORY VARIABLES

In Calculations

Typically, you create memory variables "on the fly" to hold intermediate results. Often you will use these results in later calculations.

For instance, if asked the value of Chez Jacques' inventory, we might give the command SUM COST*INVENTORY TO VALUE which creates a variable named VALUE with the numeric result contained therein. To see the contents of VALUE, we could either DISPLAY MEMORY or ? VALUE (recall that the ? is the "what is" command). Later (in the same dBASE session) we may be asked for the average inventory value per raw material. We can quickly give two commands -- COUNT TO K and ? VALUE/K -- to yield the answer.

Refer to the example in Figure 11-1. We will discuss the entries in **boldface**, which I typed. First, I used the raw material file with its index. The first item in index (logical) order is "all-beef patty," which is evident after the DISPLAY command. ? COST tells us that the cost field is 0.10.

Next, the memory variable COST is created with the command COST=COST*2 .* The result is 0.20, but when I asked dBASE ? COST , the answer was 0.10 -- the value of the field COST. To learn the value of the variable cost, I had to use the command ? M->COST .

The DISPLAY MEMORY command also tells me the value of COST, as well as how many variables are defined and available, and how many bytes are used and available. The DISPLAY command assures me that no changes have been made to the original record.

Typing -> to display memory variables is confusing and awkward, so I decide to use a different variable name. I give the command M_COST=COST*2 which creates a variable M_COST.** Note the results of the three commands ? COST , ? M->COST , and ? M_COST . A final DISPLAY MEMORY tells me that I now have two memory variables.

In Commands

Character type memory variables may also be included in commands through the use of the -- & -- macro function. For instance, if the memory variable FIELD contained the string 'first_name,last_name', then the command LIST &FIELD would be the equivalent of LIST FIRST_NAME,LAST_NAME .

Using the macro function with memory variables allows you to effectively rewrite command files as they execute. A portion of a command can be input by the user or assigned via program logic, then the macro command used to interject that portion of the command into the program. This capability will be demonstrated in Application E.

---

* In dBASE II, STORE COST*2 TO COST
** In dBASE II, I would have used m:cost

GUIDED ACTIVITY

This activity requires you to use the memory variable commands.

1. Follow the startup procedure for your version of dBASE as outlined in Unit 2.

2. Duplicate the example illustrated in Figure 11-1.

3. Compute the total raw material value (cost * quantity on hand for all items) and store the result in a variable called SUM.

✔CHECKPOINT

What command do you use to compute this sum?

_____

4. Compute the total number of items on hand and store the result in a variable called COUNT.

✔CHECKPOINT

What command do you use to compute this sum?

_____

5. Compute and print on the screen the average value per unit, i.e., SUM/COUNT. Do not create another memory variable.

✔CHECKPOINT

What command do you use to compute and print this average?

_____

6. When you have completed all of the above, give the command QUIT to exit dBASE. Remember to backup your work. If everything is proper, turn off the computer and return the dBASE software to the Lab Supervisor.

REVIEW QUESTIONS

*1. What is the difference between a variable and a field?

2. What are the types of memory variables?

3. How would you create and name the following memory variables?

   *a. a variable called NAME which contains the string 'Genghis Khan'

   *b. a variable called AGE which contains the number 16

4. What expression would you write to

   *a. add the string 'the Magnificent' to NAME

   *b. double AGE, with the result in OLDER

5. What command would you use to determine currently active memory variables?

*6. What command would you use to store all memory variables in a disk file with the filename MEMORY?

*7. What command would you use to retrieve memory variables from the disk file MEMORY, without destroying the variables currently active?

8. What command would you use to remove all memory variables from memory?

DOCUMENTATION RESEARCH

Using the reference manual, determine the answer to the following questions which deal with the commands discussed in this Unit. I recommend you also write the page number by the discussion of the command, above.

1. STORE {expression} TO {memory variable} -- how can you store the same expression to several memory variables?

2. {memory variable} = {expression} -- if the memory variable already existed, what happens with a subsequent STORE operation?

3. SAVE TO {filename} -- how do you save only some of the memory variables?

4. RESTORE FROM {filename} -- what is the effect of the ADDITIVE option?

5. DISPLAY MEMORY -- numeric variables are displayed in two ways, what are they?

6. RELEASE -- what is the function of the LIKE and EXCEPT options?

Using the reference manual, answer the following questions:

7. How many memory variables can be active at one time?

8. What is the maximum amount of memory available for memory variables?

9. What is the maximum or default length of each type of memory variable?

10. How is the & (macro function) used?

Unit

12 COMMAND FILE CREATION AND PROGRAM FLOW

The ability to program a series of steps so they can be repeated, even by persons unfamiliar with dBASE commands, is one of the major virtues of dBASE. You can, for instance, write a program to automate the production of various reports and mailing labels, or to handle the various inquiries which have been the subject of earlier units.

This unit deals with the creation of dBASE command files (programs and procedures), and the commands which control program flow. Unit 13 discusses commands for input and output, which are essential to most program operations.

LEARNING OBJECTIVES

1. At the completion of this unit you should know

   a. how command files differ from immediate mode,

   b. what a program is,

   c. what a loop is.

2. At the completion of this unit you should be able to

   a. create a command file,

   b. create a program which processes all records in a file,

   c. create a program which uses conditional logic,

   d. execute a command file.

141

IMPORTANT COMMANDS

MODIFY COMMAND {file name}
DO {file name}
CLEAR ALL
NOTE or *
DO WHILE {condition} ... ENDDO
SKIP
EXIT
LOOP
DO CASE ... CASE {condition} ... OTHERWISE ... ENDCASE
IF {condition} ... ELSE ... ENDIF
RETURN
CANCEL

COMMAND FILES VS. IMMEDIATE MODE

To this point, we have used dBASE in the immediate mode -- commands are executed as soon as we prcss <CR>, and the command is lost once it executes. With command files, the commands are stored in a disk file until we direct dBASE to execute them. Because the commands are in a disk file, we can reissue the commands several times, and we can edit the command file if necessary to correct errors or change what it does.

Following are some guidelines for when to use command files. I recommend that you build a command file whenever:

you will use a series of several commands,

you will use the same command a number of times,

you are using a complicated command, which you may have to revise several times before it does what you wish it would.

On the other hand, you would probably not use a command file if you were going to use a single, simple command once. These guidelines are not strict, however. dBASE will allow you to issue a lengthy series of commands in the immediate mode, or to put a simple command into a command file.

FILE AND RECORD FUNCTIONS

Functions in this group are primarily used in command (program) files.

BOF( ) *beginning of file function*, this is a logical function which is true if the beginning of file has been reached for the file in use. Used in conjunction with search operations.*

---

* Not available in dBASE II

```
dBASE Word Processor
```

FIGURE 12-1 The dBASE Word Processor -- New File

EOF( ) *end of file function*, this is a logical function which is true if the end of file has been reached for the file in use. Used in conjunction with search operations.*

FILE(string expression) *file function*, this is a logical function which is true if a file whose name matches the string expression exists and false otherwise. Used to determine whether or not a given file is on the disk.

RECNO( ) *the current record function*, the value of this function is the integer corresponding to the current record number.**

CREATING COMMAND FILES

A command file is a series of dBASE commands which is stored on the data disk (usually in the B: or only drive). To create such a file from within dBASE, type the command

MODIFY COMMAND {file name}

Short command files (up to 4096 bytes in length) are easily written using this command. If you do not specify an extension, dBASE will add a .PRG extension to {file name}. For command files more than 50 lines in length, you are advised to use a word processor such as WordStar.

After you type MODIFY COMMAND , the screen will clear (see Figure 12-1). You enter the command file using full screen editing keys -- the process is very similar to creating a file in most word processors. Press <CR> at the end of each command line. If the line

---

* In dBASE II, the function is EOF
** In dBASE II, the function is #

```
dBASE Word Processor
use raw_matl                                                    <
do while .not. eof()                                            <
    display                                                     <
    skip                                                        <
enddo                                                           <
```

FIGURE 12-2 The dBASE Word Processor with File
Note: Lines entered by the user are in **boldface**

is too long, dBASE will wrap the line to the next line. You may also continue a long line by typing ;<CR> (a semicolon followed by <CR>) and typing the remainder of the command on the following line. Example:

    This is an example of how you would continue a very ;
        long command onto a second line

When you are finished entering the commands, type either ^W or ^End (Ctrl-W or Ctrl-End) to exit and save. If you have made changes that you do not wish to keep, type either ^Q or Esc, and the previous version will remain the current version.

To make further changes to the file, simply issue the same MODIFY COMMAND {filename} from the . prompt. See Figure 12-2 for an example of a short command file as it appears during the modification process.

COMMANDS TO CONTROL PROGRAM FLOW

Starting a Program

The DO command is used to invoke (execute) a command file:

    DO {file name}

Unless you specify a file extension, dBASE assumes a .PRG extension. Think of all command files as subroutines, therefore DO {file name} can either initiate a program from the . prompt or can call a (sub)program from within a command file. If the program terminates with a RETURN statement, then control returns to the statement following the DO command.

dBASE III also contains a provision for procedure files. A procedure file may contain several procedures which operate in the same manner as program files. See the reference manual descriptions of PROCEDURE and SET PROCEDURE for more detail -- these commands are not covered further in this manual.

In dBASE III, memory variables created by subordinate programs/procedures are released when the program/procedure is exited, unless you make provisions for their retention. See discussions of PARAMETERS, PRIVATE, and PUBLIC in the reference manual for assistance.

Resetting dBASE. The CLEAR ALL command is used to reset dBASE.* Any open data files are unused and closed, all memory variables are released, and work area 1 is selected. It is usually a good idea to start a main program with CLEAR ALL , to insure that data or files from previous work do not contaminate your new activity.

Comments. NOTE or * as the first non-space character in a line allow comments to be placed in the command file. The comments are not normally displayed on the screen and thus are available only when the program is being edited.

The Loop

One of the fundamental aspects of almost every programming language is the loop. Loops allow the program to repeat the same instructions several times. One of the fundamental errors of programming is to create an endless loop -- one which is not programmed to end.

Starting the Loop. In dBASE, the loop is initiated by the DO WHILE command and terminated by the ENDDO command. Between these two commands are statements which are to be repeated. The fundamental structure of the loop is

```
DO WHILE {condition}
    statements
ENDDO
```

The {condition} is a logical condition (but is preceded by WHILE instead of FOR). If {condition} is a logical true, then the *statements* following the DO WHILE are executed until ENDDO is encountered. The {condition} is reevaluated and control either jumps to the statement following ENDDO (if {condition} is false) or the *statements* are executed again.

Indentation. You will notice that I indent statements within a loop. Although indentation is not necessary, it does make the program easier to read and is strongly recommended.

Exiting the Loop. There are four ways to exit a DO WHILE loop, and you must employ one or more of these to avoid endless loops:

change the value of {condition} within the loop so that is is no longer true,

---

* In dBASE II, the command is CLEAR .

the EXIT command,

the RETURN command,

the CANCEL command.

The last two commands are discussed later in this unit.

The EXIT command is used within a DO WHILE loop to transfer control to the statement immediately following the ENDDO statement.

The LOOP command is used within the body of a DO WHILE loop to skip all commands up to the ENDDO command. This causes the initiating {condition} to be reevaluated, and does not necessarily lead to an exit from the loop.

Skipping through a File

One of the primary uses of loops is to process (read, print, or change) every record in a data file. To move the record pointer to the next record and read the contents of all fields of that record, use the SKIP command. SKIP by itself will advance the pointer one record, SKIP 5 will move forward five records, and SKIP -18 will move back (toward the beginning) 18 records.

Processing All Records in a File. To process all records in a file, we normally would wish to start with the first record and proceed one record at a time until the end of the file is reached. To accomplish this, we should remember a few things. First, a file which has just been opened is positioned at the first record. Second, SKIP moves forward (toward the end of the file) and reads one record at a time. Finally, the function EOF( ) is true when we have attempted to read (i.e., SKIP) after the last record in the file.

The following program would open the file RAW_MATL, read and display each record, and terminate when the last record had been read. I suggest that you create the program and try it.

```
use raw_matl
do while .not. eof( )
    display
    skip
enddo
```

In addition to, or instead of the DISPLAY command, you could have several other commands which process each record in turn. Some of those commands are discussed in the following section.

Conditional Operations

Conditional operations allow the computer program to make some of our decisions for us. Consider the teacher who must assign grades to her class. She may have a rule such as "90 and above are A, 80-89 are B, ..." She could write a computer program which would read the numeric score and assign a letter grade based on the score. The challenge is to write the program so that it makes the decision the way we want it to.

dBASE offers two sets of conditional commands. The first, based on the IF command, is best used when there are two choices, such as true/false or male/female. The second set, based on the DO CASE command, is used when there are multiple choices, such as the teacher discussed above.

The IF Command provides a means for selecting one of two choices. The general format of the command is

```
IF {condition}
    statements
ELSE
    statements
ENDIF
```

If {condition} is true, then *statements* until ELSE (or ENDIF if there is no ELSE) will be executed. If {condition} is false, then *statements* following the ELSE (if any) will be executed. IF commands may be nested up to any level, but improperly nested commands will lead to embarrassment worse than ring around the collar.

The following program would read all items in the RAW_MATL file and display only those which had been ordered more than 10 days ago. In this case, the ELSE clause is not used.

```
use raw_matl
do while .not. eof( )
    if (date( )-last_order)>10
        display
    endif
    skip
enddo
```

The DO CASE Command is more flexible because multiple choices are accommodated in one set of statements. The general form is

```
DO CASE
    CASE {condition}
        statements
    CASE {condition}
        statements
    OTHERWISE
        statements
ENDCASE
```

DO CASE will evaluate each of the CASE {condition} until it finds one that is true, then execute the *statements* up to the next CASE {condition}, upon which it exits to ENDCASE. If none of the CASE {condition} are true, then the *statements* following OTHERWISE will be executed. Any number of CASE {condition} may be included, and the OTHERWISE statement is optional. This command is especially useful when constructing menus.

Recall the example of the teacher, who might write a program which included the following (assuming that SCORE and GRADE are fields in the file GRADEBK):

```
use gradebk
do while .not. eof( )
    do case
        case score >= 90
            replace grade with 'A'
        case score >= 80
            replace grade with 'B'
        case score >= 70
            replace grade with 'C'
        case score >= 60
            replace grade with 'D'
        otherwise
            replace grade with 'F'
    endcase
    skip
enddo
```

Once you can follow the logic of the above, answer this question: What prevents the assignment of a D to a person whose score is 75, which is greater than 60?

Exiting the Program

Three commands may be used to exit from a program or procedure. The RETURN command is used to exit a command file or a procedure and will either return to line following the DO {file name} command which called the command file or will return to the . prompt if the command file was executed directly. Normally RETURN is the last line in a command file. RETURN may also be used in conjunction with IF or DO CASE logic. The end of a command file is equivalent to a RETURN statement, i.e., command files need not end with this statement.

The CANCEL command cancels the execution of a(ll) command file(s) and returns control to the . prompt. RETURN is generally preferred, but CANCEL may be used to abort a process if something dreadful is about to occur.

QUIT may also be used in a command file to terminate the file, close all open files, and return to the operating system.

GUIDED ACTIVITY

This activity requires you to use the program creation and flow commands.

1. Follow the startup procedure for your version of dBASE as outlined in Unit 2.

2. Give the command MODIFY COMMAND SKIP , which will allow you to create a command file named SKIP.PRG . The screen should clear and look like Figure 12-1.

```
. do skip
Record#   RMID DESC                      COST  INVENTORY  LAST_ORDER
        1  0014 12 oz. cup               0.03        300  10/04/85
Record no.       2
Record#   RMID DESC                      COST  INVENTORY  LAST_ORDER
        2  0015 16 oz. cup               0.05        400  09/28/85
Record no.       3
Record#   RMID DESC                      COST  INVENTORY  LAST_ORDER
        3  0018 4 oz. fry pack           0.02        332  10/19/85
Record no.       4
Record#   RMID DESC                      COST  INVENTORY  LAST_ORDER
        4  0019 6 oz. fry pack           0.03        500  10/15/85
Record no.       5
Record#   RMID DESC                      COST  INVENTORY  LAST_ORDER
        5  0013 8 oz. cup                0.02        600  10/06/85
```

FIGURE 12-3 The SKIP Program in Progress
Note: Command entered by the user is in **boldface**

3. Enter the program shown in Figure 12-2.

4. When the program is correct, exit by typing ^W or ^End.

5. Execute the program by typing DO SKIP .

6. The program should display each record of RAW_MATL on the screen, as illustrated in Figure 12-3. If it does not, you probably made a typing error: fix it.

7. Change the program so it reads as follows:

```
use raw_matl
do while .not. eof( )
    if (date( )-last_order)>10
        display
    endif
    skip
enddo
```

8. Test the program and correct if necessary until it works.

9. When you have completed all of the above, give the command QUIT to exit dBASE. Remember to backup your work. If everything is proper, turn off the computer and return the dBASE software to the Lab Supervisor.

REVIEW QUESTIONS

1. How do command files differ from immediate mode?

*2. What is a program?

*3. What is a loop?

*4. What command do you give to create a command file?

 5. What series of commands will process all records in a file?

*6. How do you execute a command file?

DOCUMENTATION RESEARCH

Using the reference manual, determine the answer to the following questions which deal with the commands discussed in this Unit. I recommend you also write the page number by the discussion of the command, above.

1. MODIFY COMMAND {file name} -- how can you read another file into the file being edited?

2. DO {file name} -- according to the manual, how many open files may you have at one time?

3. CLEAR ALL -- what is the difference between this command and the CLOSE command?

4. NOTE or * -- what happens if the note line ends with a semicolon?

5. DO WHILE {condition} ... ENDDO -- what is the effect of comments on the ENDDO line, following the ENDDO statement?

6. SKIP -- if this command is issued when the record pointer is on the last record in a file, what is value of the functions RECNO( ) and EOF( ) ?

7. EXIT -- does this command cause the {condition} in the DO WHILE statement to be reevaluated?

8. LOOP -- does this command cause the {condition} in the DO WHILE statement to be reevaluated?

9. LOOP -- this command must be part of what other statements to function as intended?

10. DO CASE ... CASE {condition} ... OTHERWISE ... ENDCASE -- under what conditions will two CASE statements be selected?

11. IF {condition} ... ELSE ... ENDIF -- what may follow the ENDIF statement on the same line?

12. RETURN -- what is the effect of the TO MASTER option?

13. CANCEL -- what is the difference between this command and RETURN?

Unit

13 INPUT, OUTPUT, AND POSITIONING

This unit deals with the commands which move to specific points within the data file, accept data into the program, print data out of the program, and add to the data file. These commands, in conjunction with those discussed in Unit 12, provide for most of dBASE's programming utility. These commands complement the full-screen input and output commands, which are discussed in Unit 14.

LEARNING OBJECTIVES

1. At the completion of this unit you should know the differences among input, accept, and wait commands.

2. At the completion of this unit you should be able to

   a. position the record pointer to any record in the file,

   b. input string and numeric data, using prompt strings,

   c. output field and variable contents as well as short and long character strings,

   d. add a blank record to the data file,

   e. add or change information in a data file record.

IMPORTANT COMMANDS

SKIP
FIND
SEEK
LOCATE ... CONTINUE

```
GO
INPUT 'prompt' TO {memory variable}
ACCEPT 'prompt' TO {memory variable}
WAIT 'prompt' TO {memory variable}
? {expression}
?? {expression}
EJECT
CLEAR
TEXT ... ENDTEXT
APPEND BLANK
REPLACE
SET ECHO ON/OFF
SET TALK ON/OFF
SET STEP ON/OFF
SET DEBUG ON/OFF
```

MOVING ABOUT IN A DATA FILE

Most of the commands which are used to move about in the data file were introduced in earlier units. You may wish to review the section entitled "Searching through a File" in Unit 6 to refresh your memory concerning the record pointer and finding and locating records.

Move to Next Record

The SKIP command was first discussed in Unit 12. Use this command to move the record pointer forwards or backwards from its current position. Especially useful for processing the data file a record at a time.

Move Based on a Criterion

If you wish to move to a record which matches a certain criterion (e.g., the contents of a field is a certain value), then you will use one of the following commands.

The FIND command was first discussed in Unit 6. FIND is used with files that are indexed to move the record pointer to the first instance of a record that matches the index key. If there is no match, the message "NO FIND" will be displayed on the screen, and the EOF( ) function will be true. In command files, use this latter result to test for a successful find.* Often, you will wish to move to a record based on the value of a memory variable. The memory variable name is used with the & (macro function) in the FIND command. If the memory variable is named MEMVAR, then the proper command is FIND &MEMVAR .

---

* In dBASE II, if there is no match, the message "NO FIND" will be displayed on the screen, and the record number function # will give the value zero. In command files, use this latter result to test for a successful find.

In dBASE III, a variation of the FIND command is the SEEK command, which allows you to use a memory variable as the search criterion, with the command SEEK MEMVAR .

The LOCATE ... CONTINUE command set was also discussed in Unit 6. This set of commands is used to search through a file for specific values in a field or portion of a field. They are generally used when you wish to find multiple occurrences of a field value or when the search criterion is not suitable for an index key. When the record is found, the message "Record = n" is displayed and RECNO( ) equals that record. If there is no match, then "END OF FILE" is the message, EOF( ) is true, and {condition} is false.*

Move to a Specific Physical Record

The GO or GOTO command is used to position the record pointer to a specific record in the data file. To go to a specific record, say record 25, enter one of the following:

    goto record 25
    go record 25
    25

To go to the first record, use GO TOP ; to the last record, GO BOTTOM .

COMMANDS FOR DATA INPUT

Three commands are provided for the input of data into memory variables. Which you use is dependent upon the type of memory variable you wish to create.

Input to a Numeric Variable

The INPUT command may be used for input to memory variables. The general form of the command is

    INPUT "prompt" TO {memory variable}

For example:

    input 'New price: ' to newprice

This command is used in command files to enter values into memory variables. "Prompt" is optional. The memory variable is created if it did not exist before. The type of the memory variable is determined by the type of data input. If the input is delimited with ' or " or [ ] , then a character type variable is created. If the input is numeric, then a numeric variable is created. If the input is T Y F or N , then a logical variable is created.

---

* In dBASE II, when the record is found, the message "RECORD: n" is displayed and # equals that record. If there is no match, then "END OF FILE" is the message, EOF is true, and {condition} is false.

Because character data must be enclosed with quotation marks, the ACCEPT command is recommended for the entry of character data.

Input to a Character Variable

The ACCEPT command is used for input to character type memory variables. The general form of the command is

    ACCEPT "prompt" TO {memory variable}

For example:

    accept "Your name: " to name

The memory variable will be of type character regardless of what is entered. Delimiting quotation marks are not required. The "prompt" is again optional.

Input of a One-character Response

The WAIT command serves two useful functions. First, it may be used as a pause -- to suspend program operations until the user presses any key. Second, it may be used to capture a one-character response, such as a response to a menu. The two forms of the command are

    WAIT
    WAIT "prompt" TO {memory variable}

After the WAIT command, dBASE will cease all operations until a character is entered from the keyboard. In the first form, WAIT may be used as a pause, to allow the user to read what is on the screen before execution continues. In the second form, the character is stored in a memory variable. If any non-printing or control character is input then the value of the memory variable is a null (ASCII zero). Useful to capture response to a menu or to a "Do you want to do more (Y/N)?" question. For example:

    wait "Do you want to do more (Y/N)?" to answer

COMMANDS FOR OUTPUT TO THE USER

The four commands discussed in this section provide output to the user. These complement the full-screen commands which are discussed in Unit 14.

Output of a Field or Variable

The "what is" command was first discussed in Unit 4. Recall that the command consists of a question mark followed by an expression. The three forms of the command are

```
?
? {expression list}
?? {expression list}
```

This command is used to print something on the output device(s). If SET PRINT ON has been executed, then print will go to both screen and printer. The solitary ? issues a line feed and carriage return (thus printing a blank line). ? {expression list} issues a line feed and carriage return and then prints the value of {expression list}.   ?? {expression list} prints the value of {expression list} without the preceding line feed and carriage return.*

Example: suppose that you wanted to print the value of the memory variable (or data file field) FIRSTSON following an identifying legend. To do so, you would use the following:

```
? "The value of  FIRSTSON  is "
?? firstson
```

Output of a Block of Text

If you wish to output a block of text which does not contain any fields or variables, then the TEXT command may be used. The general form of the command is

```
TEXT
    lines of text
ENDTEXT
```

All of the *lines of text* will be sent to the screen (and printer if set on). This command is useful for output of a set of instructions or other information to the user.

Output on a New Screen or Page

The CLEAR command will clear the screen and home the cursor. "Home the cursor" means to move the cursor to the upper left corner of the screen.**

The EJECT command causes the printer to do a form feed -- which will move the paper to the top of the next page if the printer is set up properly.***

---

* Note to hard-core programmers: dBASE issues the line feed and carriage return (LF-CR) sequence before it prints a line rather than after -- the latter being more normal in computer languages. This can cause a problem with some parallel-interface printers which will not print a line until they receive the LF-CR. To make sure everything is printed, I recommend that you issue a solitary ? immediately after SET PRINT ON and another solitary ? immediately prior to SET PRINT OFF . This problem also exists in output commands such as LIST and DISPLAY .
** In dBASE II, the command is ERASE .
*** In dBASE II, you must SET PRINT ON before giving the EJECT command.

COMMANDS FOR OUTPUT TO THE DATA FILE

Command files generally serve one of two purposes: to extract information from data files or to add to or modify the information in a data file. To serve this latter purpose, two additional commands must be discussed.

If you are using a command file to add data to a data file, two steps must be performed. First, add a blank record to the end of the file; then replace the information in the new record with input data.

The APPEND BLANK command adds a record to the end of the data file in USE. All of the fields are blank (or 0 or false). When adding to a file via a command program, you will usually APPEND BLANK and then REPLACE FIELD1 WITH MEMVAR1, FIELD2 WITH MEMVAR2 ... and so on.

The REPLACE command was first discussed in Unit 8. This command changes value of one or more fields in one or more records of the data file. Some examples were discussed in Unit 8. In command files, you will often REPLACE a field in the current record with the contents of a memory variable:

    replace name with m__name

Example

Recall the data file DATEBOOK which was created in Unit 3. (See Figure 3-3 for the structure of that file.) To add one record to that file, we could use the following commands:

```
use datebook
append blank
accept "Name:      " to m__name
input  "Age:       " to m__age
accept "Phone:     " to m__phone
accept "Last Date: " to m__last
replace name with m__name, age with m__age, phone with m__phone ;
    last__date with ctod(m__last)
```

Note the CTOD( ) function in the REPLACE command. The variable M__LAST is character type, and must be converted to date type before the REPLACE command will work.*

In practice, these commands would probably be inside a loop which would continue as long as the user wanted to add more records.

---

* If you are using dBASE II, change the underscores [__] in variable names to colons [:], and eliminate the CTOD( ) function.

SET COMMANDS WHICH AFFECT COMMAND FILE OUTPUT

Four SET commands affect the output of command files.

SET TALK OFF will eliminate the responses that dBASE normally provides after most commands. These responses are often distracting during command file execution, and programmers use this command for a "cleaner" screen display. The effect is reversed with the SET TALK ON command. I usually set talk off at the beginning of a command file and set talk back to on just before the RETURN statement or the end of the program, which minimizes distraction during program execution while still providing feedback during the immediate mode. The commands may be issued from the immediate (dot prompt) mode or from within command files.

These commands are useful for debugging a program, i.e., locating and correcting errors:

SET ECHO ON   to display command lines as they are executed

SET TALK ON   to display intermediate results of those commands

SET STEP ON   to force the program to execute one line at a time

SET DEBUG ON   to route SET ECHO output to the printer instead of the screen

These commands may be issued from the immediate (dot prompt) mode or from within command files.

GUIDED ACTIVITY

This activity requires you to use the input and output commands.

1. Follow the startup procedure for your version of dBASE as outlined in Unit 2.

2. Write a command file using MODIFY COMMAND REPRICE which will allow you to process each record in FIN_GOOD. As each record is read, the description and selling price should be displayed on the screen. Input a new price and replace the old prices in the file with the new prices shown in Table 13-1. Before sitting down at the computer, you should outline the commands which will accomplish the following.

✔ **CHECKPOINT**
Write the commands on the lines to the right of the tasks.

a. Open the file FIN_GOOD,   _____

b. Start a loop which will continue until end of file is reached,   _____

c. Display the DESC and SELL_PRICE fields,   _____

TABLE 13-1 New Prices for Finished Goods

Description	New Selling Price	Description	New Selling Price
Apple Tarte	0.83	Large Sprite	0.85
Big Jac	1.42	Jac Meal /Co/Ap	2.35
Cheese Burger	0.72	Jac Meal /Co/Ch	2.35
Cherry Tarte	0.83	Jac Meal /Sp/Ap	2.35
Giant Coke	0.99	Jac Meal /Sp/Ch	2.35
Giant Sprite	0.99	Regular Coke	0.59
Hamburger	0.62	Regular Fries	0.47
Large Coke	0.85	Regular Sprite	0.59
Large Fries	0.70		

    d. Input the new selling price into a memory
       variable called NEW_PRICE,   _____

    e. Replace SELL_PRICE with NEW_PRICE,   _____

    f. Move forward one record,   _____

    g. Terminate the loop.   _____

3. When you have finished the program, exit from MODIFY COMMAND by typing ^W. Try the program by typing DO REPRICE -- if the program has no errors you will be able to input the new prices, as illustrated in Figure 13-1. If the program has errors, use MODIFY COMMAND REPRICE to edit, and try again.

4. After the program runs successfully, LIST TO PRINT to prove that you have made the changes.

5. TYPE REPRICE.PRG TO PRINT to make a copy of your command file.

6. Experiment with the four SET commands introduced above, giving them from the dot prompt (but do not use SET DEBUG ON if you do not have a printer). Set all four ON and execute the program, then set all four OFF and again execute the program.

7. When you have completed all of the above, give the command QUIT to exit dBASE. Remember to backup your work. If everything is proper, turn off the computer and return the dBASE software to the Lab Supervisor.

REVIEW QUESTIONS

1. What are the differences among INPUT, ACCEPT, and WAIT commands.

2. What command would you use to position the record pointer to

  *a. record 15

```
.  do reprice
Record#  desc           sell_price
     1   Apple Tarte         0.79
New Price .83
     1   record replaced
Record no.      2
Record#  desc           sell_price
     2   Big Jac             1.35
New Price 1.42
     1   record replaced
Record no.      3
Record#  desc           sell_price
     3   Cheese Burger       0.69
New Price _
```

FIGURE 13-1 The REPRICE Program in Progress
Note: Items entered by the user are in **boldface**

*b. the next record

*c. the first record whose contents is 'New York', assuming that the file is indexed on the CITY field.

3. What command would you use to input the following, using prompts:

*a. the person's name, to the variable **M_NAME**

*b. the person's age, to the variable **M_AGE**

*4. What command would you use to output the two variables input in question 3?

*5. What command is used to add a blank record to the data file?

*6. What command is used to add or change information in a data file record?

DOCUMENTATION RESEARCH

Using the reference manual, determine the answer to the following questions which deal with the commands discussed in this Unit. I recommend you also write the page number by the discussion of the command, above.

1. SKIP -- how can a memory variable be used with this command?

2. FIND -- how can a memory variable be used with this command?

3. SEEK -- how can a memory variable be used with this command?

4. LOCATE ... CONTINUE -- where is the record pointer after a successful search? after an unsuccessful search?

5. GO -- what is the alternate version of this command?

6. INPUT 'prompt' TO {memory variable} -- what happens if a <CR> is entered in response to this command?

7. ACCEPT 'prompt' TO {memory variable} -- what happens if a <CR> is entered in response to this command?

8. WAIT 'prompt' TO {memory variable} -- what happens if a <CR> is entered in response to this command?

9. ? {expression} -- find the definition of "<expression list>" in the manual. How may more than one {expression} be output with a single ? command?

10. ?? {expression} -- how does this command differ from the previous command?

11. EJECT -- what is the ASCII code for form feed?

12. CLEAR -- is it possible to clear only a portion of the screen?

13. TEXT ... ENDTEXT -- what is the effect of this command on the & (macro) function?

14. APPEND BLANK -- where is the record pointer after this command is executed?

15. REPLACE -- what is the problem with making multiple replacements on an indexed field?

16. SET ECHO ON/OFF -- what is the normal state of this command?

17. SET TALK ON/OFF -- what is the normal state of this command?

18. SET STEP ON/OFF -- when stepping is on, what key leads to the next step, and what key will cancel the process?

19. SET DEBUG ON/OFF -- what is the normal state of this command?

Unit

14 CUSTOM INPUT AND OUTPUT FORMS

In this unit we introduce the commands which are used to develop custom input and output forms. This set of commands will allow you to create professional appearing forms for data entry and to precisely format output from your application.

LEARNING OBJECTIVES

1. At the completion of this unit you should understand the concept of screen addressing.

2. At the completion of this unit you should be able to

   a. output field or variable data anywhere on the screen,

   b. create a form for data input.

IMPORTANT COMMANDS

> @ ... SAY
> @ ... GET
> READ
> SET DEVICE TO ...
> SET FORMAT TO ...

FULL SCREEN ADDRESSING

The standard personal computer screen is eighty (80) columns wide and twenty five (25) rows high. The columns are numbered 0 (zero) to 79, the rows 0 to 24. 0,0 is the upper left corner, 24,79 is the lower right. dBASE will allow you to position the output anywhere within those screen dimensions through the use of the @ command. The @ command can also be used to format output to be sent to the printer.

Full Screen Output

The command for full screen output is the @ SAY command. The simple form of the command is

@ *x,y* SAY {expression}

which will write an expression (character string, memory variable, or field) at row *x*, column *y*. You may write more than one expression to the same row, and it is not necessary to write the expressions in row-order if you are writing to the screen. That is, the first write may be to row 5, and a later write may be to row 2. If you are writing to the printer (see "Output device," below), the rows must be written in ascending order.

An example of several @ SAY commands appears in Figure 14-1. These should be self-explanatory, except for the one which reads @ 16,10 SAY 'Cost: '+STR(COST,8,2) . dBASE will allow only one type of data in a given @ SAY command, therefore it was necessary to use the STR( ) function to convert the numeric field COST to a string. Where the field is used by itself, as in @ 13,60 SAY COST , then no conversion is necessary.

More precisely formatted output is obtained with a PICTURE {format} specification.* It is possible to embed commas and leading $ or * signs. The command then would take the following form:

@ *x,y* SAY {expression} PICTURE {format}

The format characters used with @ SAY are

    !   converts all alpha characters to upper case
    $ displays dollar signs in place of leading zeros
    *   displays asterisks in place of leading zeros
    .   position of decimal point
    ,   position of comma

PICTURE formats are discussed in the dBASE manual with the @ command. Example:

@ 5,5 say cost picture '$,$$$,$$$.$$'

---

* In dBASE II, the format specification is USING {format}:

@ *x,y* SAY {expression} USING {format}

```
. find 0001
. display
      8  0001 all-beef patty        0.10 100 10/01/85
. @ 6,0 say desc

all-beef patty
. @ 10,30 say 'Desc: '+desc


                              Desc: all-beef patty
. @ 13,60 say cost


                                                              0.10
. @ 16,10 say 'Cost: '+str(cost,8,2)

          Cost:       0.10
. @ 22,30 say 'Full Screen Output Example'




                         Full Screen Output Example

. _
```

FIGURE 14-1 Example of Full Screen Output
Note: Items entered by the user are in **boldface**

Output Device

The output of @ SAY is normally directed to the screen. To change the output to the
printer, give the command SET DEVICE TO PRINT. To change back to screen output, give
the command SET DEVICE TO SCREEN. When output is directed to the printer, the rows
must be output in order. Whenever a row with a number lower than the previously printed
row is encountered, the printer will do a page eject (form feed).

Full Screen Input

The command for full screen input is the @ GET command. The simple form of the command
is

    @ x,y GET {expression}
        more @ ... GET commands may be given
    READ

The {expression} may be either a character-type memory variable or a data file field of any type. Before getting a memory variable, the variable size and (character) type must have been specified using either STORE or RESTORE commands. The current value of the variable or field is displayed at row *x*, column *y*, and the user enters a new value or accepts the old value by typing <CR>.

The GET command is not active until a subsequent READ is encountered. Once the READ command is given, then the user moves from input field to input field, entering data, much as in the APPEND operation. Full-screen cursor control keys are usable here, see Unit 2 of this manual.

It is possible to limit the input to numbers only, to convert input letters to upper case, and also to embed specific characters at specific bytes with the PICTURE {format} specification. The format characters used with @ GET are

9	allows only digits for character data, digits and signs for numeric data
#	allows only digits, blanks, and signs
A	allows only letters
L	allows only logical data
N	allows letters and digits
X	allows any character
!	converts all input alpha characters to upper case

Other characters in the {format} are accepted as is. For instance, the command to input telephone numbers might be

    @ 5,4 get tel_numb picture '(999)999-9999'

which would allow only numbers, and automatically place the parentheses and hyphen. PICTURE formats are discussed in the dBASE manual with the @ command.

In dBASE III, @ GET may also check for range of numeric input data, e.g.,

    @ 9,9 get grade range 0,4

Combining Output and Input

The @ SAY and GET commands may be combined for prompted input:

    @ 5,4 say 'Telephone ' get tel_numb picture '(999)999-9999'

which will write the word "Telephone" at row 5, column 4 and then display the picture format at row 5, column 15.

Erasing Part of the Screen

To erase part of the screen, use one of the following

    @ *x,y* CLEAR   to erase screen below and to right of row *x* column *y*

@ x,y   to erase row x from column y to right side

e.g., @ 5,5 will erase row five from column five to 79.

Changing the Default Screen Format

By now you are familiar with the standard dBASE format for edit and append operations. It is possible to create a special file, with a .FMT extension, of @ SAY and @ GET commands which will be used by dBASE instead of the standard format for EDIT and APPEND. Once created, the default is changed with the following command:

SET FORMAT TO {format filename}

The format file is created using MODIFY COMMAND or other editors, such as dFORMAT and SED which are furnished with various versions of dBASE.

GUIDED ACTIVITY

This activity requires you to use the full screen input and output commands.

1. Follow the startup procedure for your version of dBASE as outlined in Unit 2.

2. Write a command file using MODIFY COMMAND REPRICE2 which will allow you to process each record in FIN_GOOD. As each record is read, the description and selling price should be displayed on the screen. Input a new price and replace the old prices in the file with the new prices shown in Table 14-1. This program should use the full screen input and output commands. Before sitting down at the computer, you should outline the commands which will accomplish the following.

✔ **CHECKPOINT**
Write the commands on the lines to the right of the tasks.

a. Open the file FIN_GOOD,   _____

b. Start a loop which will continue until end
   of file is reached,   _____

c. Clear the screen,   _____

d. Output the DESC field at row 5, column 5,   _____

e. Input the new price at row 7, column 5,   _____
   (two commands)

                                                             _____

f. Move forward one record,   _____

g. Terminate the loop.   _____

TABLE 14-1 New Prices for Finished Goods

Description	New Selling Price	Description	New Selling Price
Apple Tarte	0.84	Large Sprite	0.85
Big Jac	1.45	Jac Meal /Co/Ap	2.45
Cheese Burger	0.77	Jac Meal /Co/Ch	2.45
Cherry Tarte	0.83	Jac Meal /Sp/Ap	2.45
Giant Coke	0.99	Jac Meal /Sp/Ch	2.45
Giant Sprite	0.99	Regular Coke	0.59
Hamburger	0.65	Regular Fries	0.49
Large Coke	0.85	Regular Sprite	0.59
Large Fries	0.70		

3. When you have finished the program, exit from MODIFY COMMAND by typing ^W. Try the program by typing DO REPRICE2 -- if the program has no errors you will be able to input the new prices as illustrated in Figure 14-2. (Some of the prices are changed from those which you input in Unit 13, some are the same.) If the program has errors, use MODIFY COMMAND REPRICE2 to edit, and try again.

4. After the program runs successfully, LIST TO PRINT to prove that you have made the changes. Then TYPE REPRICE2.PRG TO PRINT to make a copy of your command file.

5. When you have completed all of the above, give the command QUIT to exit dBASE. Remember to backup your work. If everything is proper, turn off the computer and return the dBASE software to the Lab Supervisor.

REVIEW QUESTIONS

1. What is meant by screen addressing?

*2. What is the address of the upper right corner of the screen?

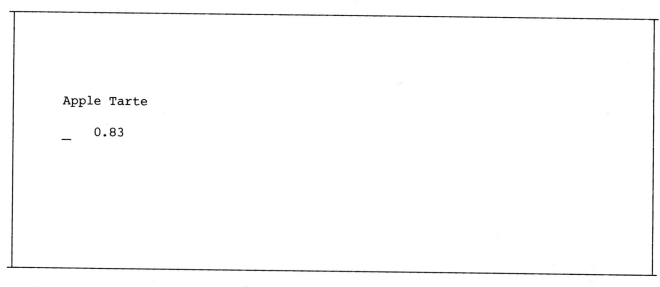

```
    Apple Tarte

 _     0.83
```

FIGURE 14-2 The REPRICE2 Program in Progress

DOCUMENTATION RESEARCH

Using the reference manual, determine the answer to the following questions which deal with the commands discussed in this Unit. I recommend you also write the page number by the discussion of the command, above.

1. @ ... SAY -- what are functions in the PICTURE option?

2. @ ... GET -- if you are using this command to input dollars and cents, what must be in the PICTURE template?

3. READ -- what is the relationship of this command to the CLEAR command?

Application

E ED & BRUCE SPECIALTIES (II)

This application exercise requires you to build a command file to revise the E&BS mailing list.

1. Follow the startup procedure for your version of dBASE as outlined in Unit 2.

2. As you may recall, E&BS has a file called MAILING.DBF which contains information concerning products ordered by their customers. (See Application D.) As customers order products, the file has been updated by editing the customer records.

   The edit process is dreadfully slow, however, and E&BS has been keeping lists of who has ordered which products (see Tables E-1, E-2, and E-3).

3. You have been asked to write a command file which will help automate the procedure. The command file should do the following:

   a. Ask the user which type of product is to be updated,

   b. Open the file MAILING,

   c. Start a loop which will continue until the end of file is reached,

   d. Clear the screen,

   e. Output the FIRST_NAME field at row 8, column 10 and the LAST_NAME field at row 8, column 21,

   f. Input the value of the appropriate field (CLOTHES, GADGETS, or SP_FOOD) at row 10, column 20,

   g. Move forward one record,

TABLE E-1   Persons Who have ordered Clothes

First Name	Last Name
Lillian	Forget
Tillie	Gillespie
Carla	Hasenzahl
David	Hoang
Robert	Kipp
Jessica	Lowe
Mary Kay	Moser
Mary	Prucha
Khosrow	Sheikh
Laura	Streich
Sharon	Tackes
George	Wood
Michael	Ziebert

    h. Terminate the loop.

4. Most of the above should be easy by now, but steps a. and f. are a bit tricky. We want to make this program general enough to update each of the three logical fields, one at a time. Therefore, we must know which field is to be updated, and write the command in f. to accept any of the field names. In a., you will need a menu which allows the user to indicate which of the three types of purchase is to be updated. You may create the menu with the following set of commands:

```
m_choice='0'
do while .not. m_choice$'123'
    clear
    text
    Which type of purchase are you updating:

    1   Clothes

    2   Tools and Gadgets

    3   Specialty Foods

    endtext
    wait '    Enter 1, 2, or 3 .. ' to m_choice
enddo
```

which will capture the user's choice in a memory variable called M_CHOICE. The first statement is used to create and initialize M_CHOICE. A variable must be created before it may be used in a {condition} or @ ... GET statement. The remainder of the statements are designed to allow only a valid entry. You should ponder the rationale behind the DO WHILE loop, which is called an error trapping routine.

TABLE E-2 Persons Who have ordered Tools and Gadgets

First Name	Last Name
Karrie	Asselin
Ralph	Blumenthal
Audie	Brueckman
Vilis	Cahill
Fred	Davis
Lois	Farley
Joyce	Fromstein
Mary Pat	Gritzmacher
Grace	Huckstep
Donna	Ladish
Kenneth	Melsheimer
Kenneth	O'Malley
Jack	Oswald
Stephanie	Weber
Linda	Wild

Once the choice is captured, you will have to assign the proper field name to a memory variable, which will be referenced in step f. The following DO CASE logic should follow the commands above:

```
do case
    case m_choice='1'
        m_field='CLOTHES'
    case m_choice='2'
        m_field='GADGETS'
    case m_choice='3'
        m_field='SP_FOOD'
endcase
```

Finally, in step f., you may use the variable M_FIELD in the @ GET command:

```
@ 10,20 get &m_field
read
```

This command uses the macro function -- & -- to substitute the contents of a character-type memory variable (M_FIELD) into a command.

5. The remainder of the program is up to you. Create the program under the name REVISE and test it until it works. When it does work properly, use the program to enter the data from the three tables (which will require you to execute the program three times). When you execute the program, you will be presented with the names and the current value of the field (see Figure E-1). If the current value is False and the name appears in the table, then change the name to True by pressing the letter T. If the current value is already True, or if the current value is False and the name does not appear in the table, then press <CR> to move to the next record.

```
Donna        Boyd

             T
```

FIGURE E-1 The REVISE Program in Operation

6. As you work with this program, think of ways to make it more efficient from the user's point of view. Is there any way to eliminate the need to go through all records in the file each time you update records? Is there a way to skip those records which already have a True for the field in question? What other improvements would you suggest?

7. When you are finished with this exercise, QUIT to exit dBASE. Remember to backup your work, then turn off the computer and return the dBASE software to the Lab Supervisor.

TABLE E-3 Persons Who have ordered Specialty Foods

First Name	Last Name
Richard	Caulker
Lillian	Forget
Deborah	Helbert
Eileen	Kotnik
Marcia	Pate
Laura	Streich

15 MULTIPLE FILES

This unit is devoted to a discussion of the use of multiple files in dBASE. With dBASE II, you may have two files open at once. With dBASE III, you may have ten files open. In either case, there are fairly simple methods for juggling the open files to gain needed information.

LEARNING OBJECTIVES

1. At the completion of this unit you should know

   a. what a work area is,

   b. what an alias is,

   c. the difference between the selected work area and other open work areas.

2. At the completion of this unit you should be able to

   a. open multiple files,

   b. read field contents of any open file,

   c. write data to any field in any open file.

IMPORTANT COMMANDS

SELECT
USE
FIND
SEEK

OPENING MULTIPLE FILES

dBASE allows the use of multiple files by assigning each to a different work area. A work area is a logical concept, and we need not be concerned with exactly how dBASE manages work areas. Consider a work area to be like a hotel room: there is only one occupant (data file) per room, the occupant may change, we can reach the present occupant by calling the room number, we can only visit one room at a time, and a given occupant can be in only one room at a time.

dBASE III allows you to have data files open in up to ten different work areas: 1 through 10 (or A through J). dBASE II allows two files: Primary and Secondary. The SELECT command is used to indicate which work area is to be used in subsequent operations. It is possible to use fields in any file, regardless of which work area is selected. The general form of the command is

> SELECT n
> > *where n = 1 to 10, or A, B, C, ... J*   *(dBASE III)*
> > *where n = PRIMARY or SECONDARY*   *(dBASE II)*

which selects one of the work areas for future operations. Records and fields in all areas are available for input. Output (i.e., REPLACE ...) is to the file in the selected work area only. Positioning (e.g., GOTO, SKIP, etc.) affects only the selected file, unless SET RELATION is activated (see Unit 16).

Files are specified as follows. When dBASE is loaded, or after a CLEAR ALL, the primary (A) area is active. Any file used at this time will be the primary file. Start a command file with the following sample commands if you want both first and second work areas active:*

> clear all
> use primfile
> select b
> use secofile
> > *any statements here will affect secondary file*
> select a
> > *any statements here will affect primary file*
> select b
> use difffile
> > *a different secondary file is used*
> > > *and the previous secondary file is closed*
> > *any statements here will affect the new*
> > > *secondary file*

---

* In dBASE II, replace all "select b" statements with "select secondary" and all "select a" statements with "select primary"

ALIASES AND PREFIXES

To refer to fields in files (work areas) other than the currently selected area, it is necessary to use aliases or prefixes. The procedure varies slightly depending on which version you are using.

In dBASE III

As mentioned above, fields from any work area data file may be used in expressions. Fields in files other than the currently selected must be referred to by aliases. The alias may be specified in the USE command:

    use difffile alias df

If no alias is specified, then the file name and the work area are interchangeable as the alias. Aliases may be upper or lower case, and do not count as part of the 10-character limit for field names.

The alias is combined with the field name as follows:

    alias->field_name

where the "arrow" is a combination of the hyphen and the greater than sign. The following are legitimate field references:

df->name	*the field NAME in a data file used with alias DF*
b->age	*the field AGE in a data file used in the second work area*
primfile->sex	*the field SEX in a data file named PRIMFILE*

In dBASE II

As mentioned above, fields from either primary or secondary data file may be used in expressions. If the field name is duplicated (the same field name occurs in both files) then the prefixes P. and S. are used for differentiating the fields. (I make a habit of using P. and S. anyway, one never knows how the files may be changed in the future.) The P. and S. prefixes may be upper or lower case, and do not count as part of the 10-character limit for field names.

The following are legitimate field references:

p.name	*the field NAME in the data file in the primary work area*
s.age	*the field AGE in the data file in the secondary work area*

MULTIPLE FILE OPERATIONS

There are many possible multiple file operations, several of which are discussed in this and the following units.

One of the first uses which people make of multiple files is to look up data in a second file based on information in the first file. This is usually accomplished by indexing the second file on some key expression which also appears in the primary file. As data are entered into the primary file, the secondary file is checked for relevant information.

For instance, assume that a store has a list of all customers and their credit limits in a file which is indexed on customer number. As orders are entered into an orders file, the credit file is checked to insure that the order total does not exceed the credit limit.

As another example, a file of two-letter state abbreviations, minimum and maximum zip code values, and full state names may exist to assist in an address-entry application. This file would be indexed on state abbreviation. As an address is entered, the abbreviation is checked against the abbreviations list, the zip code is checked against the minimum and maximum allowable for that state, and the full state name is displayed as a check for the operator.

In each of these cases, the FIND (or SEEK in dBASE III) command is used to link the two files. When the key expression is entered, dBASE attempts to find the match in the other file. For instance, if the state abbreviation is entered into a memory variable called M_ABBR and the check file is in the second work area, then the following would be used:*

```
select 2
seek m_abbr
select 1
```

Note that the second work area must be selected prior to the search, and that the primary area is re-selected after the search.

If there is a find (e.g., the customer number in the credit file), then the checking proceeds. If there is no find, then the operator is informed that some error has been made. Also, if the other items are not as specified (e.g., credit limit exceeded), then another type of error message is presented to the operator.

Additional multiple file operations are discussed in the following units.

---

* In dBASE II, the commands would be

```
select secondary
find &m:abbr
select primary
```

GUIDED ACTIVITY

This activity requires you to use two data files.

1. Follow the startup procedure for your version of dBASE as outlined in Unit 2.

2. Write a command file called LOOKUP which will compute the cost of raw materials in a given Chez Jacques menu item. The program should accept a FGID as input, read through the MIX file for all records which match that FGID. For each match, the program should locate the corresponding RMID in the RAW_MATL file, multiply the RM_QTY in MIX times the COST in RAW_MATL, and keep a running sum. When no more matches with the FGID are found, the sum should be printed and the program should terminate. Before sitting down at the computer, you should outline the commands which will accomplish the following.

✔CHECKPOINT

Write the commands on the lines to the right of the tasks.

a. Open the file MIX, _____

b. Index MIX on FGID, _____

c. Select second work area, _____

d. Open the file RAW_MATL, _____

e. Index RAW_MATL on RMID, _____

f. Select primary work area, _____

g. Set a memory variable called TOTCOST to 0 (zero), _____

h. Input the FGID, _____

i. Find the first match in MIX, _____

j. Start a loop which will continue until the FGID in the MIX file does not match the input FGID, _____

k. Select secondary work area, _____

l. Find the record in RAW_MATL that matches the RMID in the MIX file record, _____

m. Select the primary work area, _____

n. Multiply RM_QTY in MIX file times COST in RAW_MATL file and add to TOTCOST, _____

o. Move to the next record in MIX, _____

```
. do lookup
mix.ndx already exists, overwrite it? (Y/N) Yes
      82 records indexed
raw_matl.ndx already exists, overwrite it? (Y/N) Yes
      19 records indexed
0
Enter FGID 1007
          0.10
Record no.       61
          0.16
Record no.       62
          0.26
Record no.       63
          0.30
Record no.       64
          0.32
Record no.       65
          0.32

. _
```

FIGURE 15-1 The LOOKUP Program in Operation
Note: Items entered by the user are in **boldface**

    p. Terminate the loop,   _____

    q. Print the result.   _____

3. When you have finished the program, exit from modify command and test the program by typing DO LOOKUP and entering various valid FGIDs. (See example in Figure 15-1.) If the program does not operate properly, revise and test again.

4. TYPE LOOKUP.PRG TO PRINT to make a copy of the program.

5. When you have completed all of the above, give the command QUIT to exit dBASE. Remember to backup your work. If everything is proper, turn off the computer and return the dBASE software to the Lab Supervisor.

REVIEW QUESTIONS

1. What is a work area?

2. What is an alias?

3. What is the difference between the selected work area and other open work areas?

4. Assume that a file named SOX is open in the second work area, that the file INDIANS is open in the primary (first) work area, and that the primary work area is currently selected. How would you compute and display the following:

  *a. the sum of the field RED in the SOX file and CLEVELAND in the INDIANS file,

  * b. the difference between RED in the SOX file and WHITE in the SOX file.

*5. Continuing the situation in question 4, how would you place the number 200 in the field RED in the SOX file? (Two commands are needed.)

DOCUMENTATION RESEARCH

Using the reference manual, determine the answer to the following questions which deal with the commands discussed in this Unit. I recommend you also write the page number by the discussion of the command, above.

1. SELECT -- under what condition would the command SELECT P work in dBASE III?

2. USE -- what will be the alias if none is specified?

Unit

16 RELATIONAL DATA BASE OPERATIONS

In this unit we provide an introduction to relational data base operations using dBASE. Because the relational capabilities of dBASE II are rather limited, the discussion will focus on dBASE III.

Relational data base operations are those operations in which one data file is linked, via a key value, to another data file. A movement in one of the data files will cause a corresponding movement in the other data file. Relational operations are very useful in creating sophisticated applications involving diverse kinds of data.

LEARNING OBJECTIVES

1. At the completion of this unit you should know what a relation is.

2. At the completion of this unit you should be able to establish a relation between two files.

IMPORTANT COMMANDS

SET RELATION TO {key expression} INTO {alias}
SET RELATION TO {numeric expression} INTO {alias}

CONCEPTS OF RELATIONAL OPERATIONS

A relational data base is one in which various tables are linked together via key expressions. Although there is some debate in the professional community as to whether or not dBASE is a true relational data base management system, its capabilities are very similar to a relational DBMS.

dBASE uses the term "data file" instead of the more common terms "table" or "relation." Either term refers to a row X column matrix of data, such as the data files we have used throughout this manual.

Relation Defined

A relation is a link between two data files (such as dBASE .DBF files). As the record pointer is moved in one file, the record pointer in the other file is moved to a corresponding record. In dBASE, relations are established via key expressions and indexes. The method for linking will be discussed later in this unit.

Types of Relations

There are three types of relations which may be established. The type of relation is important because it affects the method of linking the files together. These types parallel the traditional family structure, which is used as an example.

One to One (1:1) Relation. A husband and wife are in a 1:1 relationship -- a husband has (no more than) one wife, and a wife has (no more than) one husband. In a 1:1 relation, there may be no match for a given case, e.g., a wife with out a husband (i.e., divorced or widowed), but there may not be more than one match for a given case (e.g., a wife with many husbands).

Another example of a 1:1 relation is states and capital cities.

Where a 1:1 relation exists, the files may be directly linked such that a (record pointer) movement in one results in a movement to the corresponding record in the other.

One to Many (1:M) Relation. A mother and her children are in a 1:M relation -- each mother may have many children, but each child may have only one mother. The "one" (mother) file may have zero, one, or several matches with the "many" (child) file, but the "many" file may have only zero or one match with the "one" file.

Another example of a 1:M relation is the state abbreviation verification example discussed in Unit 15. A given state may appear in many different addresses, but a given address is in only one state.

Where a 1:M relation exists, the "many" file may be directly linked to the "one" file such that a movement in the former (child) results in a movement to the corresponding record in the latter (mother). The reverse is not true, however. The "one" file may be linked to the "many" file such that a movement in the "one" file leads to a movement to one of the matching records in the "many" file, the remainder of the matches in the "many" file must be found by some other method. Typically, the "many" file is indexed on the key used to match the two, and the second and succeeding matches will be the following (logical) records.

Many to Many (N:M) Relation. Parents and children are in a N:M relation -- each parent may have many children, and each child may have many (i.e., two) parents. Either file may have zero, one, or many matches with the other file.

Another example of a N:M relation is the Chez Jacques menu and raw materials application in this manual.

Where a N:M relation exists, the files are linked through an intermediate file called a link file such as the MIX.DBF file. This file contains keys to both of the files (i.e., FGID, RMID) as well as information unique to the intersection (e.g., the RM_QTY, which is the amount of the specific raw material in the specific menu item).

ESTABLISHING RELATIONS

Relations are established with the SET RELATION command, which is unique to dBASE III. The general forms of the command are

    SET RELATION TO {key expression} INTO {alias}
    SET RELATION TO {numeric expression} INTO {alias}

which will cause all sequential commands to perform positioning on both selected and alias data files. That is, whenever a record pointer movement is made in the selected ("from") file, the record pointer in the alias ("to") file is moved to the corresponding record. You may then make other movements in the "to" file and these do not affect the "from" file. Up to ten relations may exist at one time, but no more than one relation from any given file.

To establish a relation, both files must have been opened (in two different work areas). The work area of the "from" file must be selected when the SET RELATION command is given.

If {numeric expression} is used, the {alias} file will be positioned to the record number matching the expression. The {alias} file must not be indexed (or, opened with an index).

The {key expression} alternative is more often used because no assumptions need be made about the physical order of the {alias} file. If {key expression} is used, the {alias} file must be indexed on that key. For instance, two files might have ID number fields. The following would establish a relation such that any movement in FIRST would cause the record pointer to move to the corresponding ID number in SECOND.

    clear all
    select a
    use first
    select b
    use second index second alias two
    select a
    set relation to id into two

This method is much easier than the SELECT ... SEEK ... SELECT syntax described in Unit 15. Whenever the record pointer is moved in FIRST, dBASE performs the equivalent of SELECT ... SEEK ... SELECT to move the record pointer in SECOND to the appropriate record, without any programming to that effect.

USING RELATIONS

This section contains three examples of how relations may be used. For these examples, assume that you have two files, WIVES and HUSBANDS, that each is indexed as noted below (with no duplicates, i.e., there are not two husbands with the name 'John Smith'), and that each has the same structure:

Field	Field name	Type	Width	Dec
1	LAST_NAME	Character	15	
2	FIRST_NAME	Character	10	
3	SPOUSE_LN	Character	15	
4	SPOUSE_FN	Character	10	
5	AGE	Numeric	2	
6	INCOME	Numeric	6	

You have already given the following commands

```
clear all
use husbands
index on upper(last_name+first_name) to husbands
select b
use wives
index on upper(last_name+first_name) to wives
set relation to upper(spouse_ln+spouse_fn) into husbands
```

As you read the examples which follow, remember that the relation is established from the B (WIVES) file to the A (HUSBANDS) file.

Note that the {key expression} -- UPPER(SPOUSE_LN+SPOUSE_FN) -- does not have to use the same field names as the {index key} -- UPPER(LAST_NAME+FIRST_NAME) -- but the contents of the expressions must be the same. For instance, the record for me in the HUSBANDS file would have 'Ross   ' as LAST_NAME and 'Steven   ' as FIRST_NAME. The record for my wife in WIVES should have 'Ross   ' as SPOUSE_LN and 'Steven   ' as SPOUSE_FN. If so, then the relation will point to my record in HUSBANDS whenever the pointer is moved to her record in WIVES. All expressions have been converted to upper case to remove any inconsistencies in capitalization in the two files.

Computing

To compute total family income of a given family, move the record pointer to the wife's record (which will move the pointer to the corresponding husband's record) and give the command

```
? a->income+b->income
```

which adds the INCOME field from both A (HUSBANDS) and B (WIVES) files and displays the result.

Reporting

Reports may also refer to related files. Establish the relation as above prior to defining the report (MODIFY REPORT command). If you exit dBASE or change the relations, you will also have to establish the relation prior to executing the report (REPORT FORM command).

Report columns may contain fields from the alias file (e.g., A->AGE in a column entitled 'Husband Age') and also computations (e.g., A->INCOME+B->INCOME as in the example above).

Listing

The LIST and DISPLAY commands may also refer to fields in the related file. For instance, you might give the command

    list off last_name,spouse_ln,age,a->age for (last_name)<>(spouse_ln)

to obtain a list of the ages of all couples who do not share the same last name.

GUIDED ACTIVITY

This activity requires you to establish and use a relationship between two files. You must use dBASE III to accomplish this activity.

1. Follow the startup procedure for your version of dBASE as outlined in Unit 2.

2. Write a command file called RELATE which will compute the cost of raw materials in a given Chez Jacques menu item. The program should accept a FGID as input, read through the MIX file for all records which match that FGID. For each match, the program should locate the corresponding RMID in the RAW_MATL file, multiply the RM_QTY in MIX times the COST in RAW_MATL, and keep a running sum. When no more matches with the FGID are found, the sum should be printed and the program should terminate.

    This is virtually the same program as that you created in Unit 15, except that you should set a relation between MIX and RAW_MATL instead of using the SEEK command. Before sitting down at the computer, outline the commands which will accomplish the following.

✔CHECKPOINT
Write the commands on the lines to the right of the tasks.

a. Open the file MIX, _____

b. Index MIX on FGID, _____

c. Select second work area, _____

```
. do relate
mix.ndx already exists, overwrite it? (Y/N) Yes
     82 records indexed
raw_matl.ndx already exists, overwrite it? (Y/N) Yes
     19 records indexed
0
Enter FGID 1006
          0.10
Record no.        57
          0.16
Record no.        58
          0.26
Record no.        59
          0.30
Record no.        60
          0.30

. _
```

FIGURE 16-1 The RELATE Program in Operation
Note: Items typed by user are in **boldface**

d. Open the file RAW_MATL, _____

e. Index RAW_MATL on RMID, _____

f. Select primary work area, _____

g. Set a relation to RAW_MATL based on RMID, _____

h. Set a memory variable called TOTCOST to 0 (zero), _____

i. Input the FGID, _____

j. Find the first match in MIX, _____

k. Start a loop which will continue until the FGID
    in the MIX file does not match the input FGID, _____

l. Multiply RM_QTY in MIX file times COST in
    RAW_MATL file and add to TOTCOST, _____

m. Move to the next record in MIX, _____

n. Terminate the loop, _____

o. Print the result. _____

3. When you have finished the program, exit from modify command and test the program by typing DO RELATE and entering various valid FGIDs. (See illustration in Figure 16-1.) If the program does not operate properly, revise and test again.

4. TYPE RELATE.PRG TO PRINT to make a copy of the program.

5. When you have completed all of the above, give the command QUIT to exit dBASE. Remember to backup your work. If everything is proper, turn off the computer and return the dBASE software to the Lab Supervisor.

REVIEW QUESTIONS

*1. What is a relation?

2. List the three types of relations, and give an example of each.

DOCUMENTATION RESEARCH

Using the reference manual, determine the answer to the following question which deals with the command discussed in this Unit. I recommend you also write the page number by the discussion of the command, above.

SET RELATION TO ... -- how is the relation disconnected?

Unit

17 OTHER MULTIPLE FILE OPERATIONS

In this final unit, we discuss additional multiple file commands. One of the commands is used to update one file based on information contained in another file. The second command is used to create a new file based on the associations between the information contained in two source files. This unit also contains a discussion of a command which is used to create a data file of summary information.

LEARNING OBJECTIVES

1. At the completion of this unit you should know

    a. what an update operation is,

    b. what a join operation is.

2. At the completion of this unit you should be able to

    a. update one data file based on information contained in another,

    b. join two files to create a third based on some logical relationship between the two files,

    c. create a file containing subtotals of the data in another file.

IMPORTANT COMMANDS

    UPDATE ON {key} FROM {alias} REPLACE {field} WITH {expression} RANDOM
    JOIN WITH {alias} TO {file} FOR {condition}
    TOTAL ON {key} TO {data file}

UPDATING A DATA FILE

Updating is the process of changing the information in one file based on the information contained in another. You performed updates manually in Units 13 and 14, when you entered new prices in the menu file. This section tells you how to perform the same operation automatically.

The general forms of the UPDATE command are

UPDATE ON {key} FROM {alias} REPLACE {field} WITH {expression}
UPDATE ON {key} FROM {alias} REPLACE {field} WITH {expression} RANDOM

which changes the information in the selected file based on the information in {alias} file, which is a dBASE data file.

Both files must be sorted or indexed on {key}, unless the RANDOM qualifier is used. RANDOM allows the FROM file to be in any order but the selected file must be indexed on {key}. The {key} field must be the same (name, type, width) in both data files.

If the WITH {expression} involves fields from the {alias} file (which is usually the case), those fields must be referred to by their alias.

For example, assume that you have two files, INVENTOR.DBF and CHANGES.DBF -- with new prices in the latter. Both files have PART_NO and PRICE fields, and you want to update the INVENTOR file with information from CHANGES. INVENTOR is indexed on PART_NO.

```
clear all
use inventor
index on part_no to inventor
select b
use changes
select a
update on part_no from b replace price with b->price random
```

Note that the file to be updated is selected prior to the update operation. Study this example carefully, for you will be expected to perform a similar operation in the guided activity for this unit.

CREATION OF A FILE OF RELATIONS

Joining is the process of merging fields from two files to create a third file. The command used is the JOIN command:

JOIN WITH {alias} TO {file} FOR {condition}

which uses two databases to create a third whenever some condition is met.*

---

* The JOIN procedure in dBASE II is similar, but there are slight differences.

JOIN goes to the first (logical) record in the selected data file and evaluates each record in the alias data file against that record. Whenever the {condition} is true, a record is output to the TO file. After each record in the alias file has been evaluated, the selected file is advanced one record and the process repeats -- until all selected file records have been evaluated. JOIN takes a long time to complete. If there are 1000 records in each file, then 1,000,000 comparisons must be made.

Note that the potential output of this procedure is the product of the number of records in the selected file times the number of records in the alias file. Thus if each file had 1000 records, and {condition} was always true, then 1000 records would be output for each record in the selected file. 1000 * 1000 = 1,000,000

The output file will consist of the FIELDS specified or, if the FIELDS specification is not present, will consist of all selected file fields and as many of the alias file fields as will fit.* Alias file fields must be referred to with the ALIAS->FIELD_NAME syntax.

An example (dBASE III):

```
clear all
select a
use first
select b
use second alias two
select a
join with two to new for id=two->id
```

will create a file called NEW.DBF with fields from both FIRST and SECOND. A record will be output for every match of ID numbers. If an ID number exists in one file but not the other, no record will be output.

CREATION OF A FILE OF SUBTOTALS

The TOTAL command is used to compute subtotals of numeric fields and place those subtotals in a separate data file. The subtotals are computed for distinct groups of data, based on a key field. The general forms of the command are

```
TOTAL ON {key} TO {data file}
TOTAL ON {key} TO {data file} FIELDS {list} FOR {condition}
```

The {key} field must be a character type field for the command to function properly. The open data base must be either sorted or indexed on the {key} field before the TOTAL command is given. All records with the same {key} value become a single record in the TO {data file}. Numeric type fields named in the FIELDS {list} (which is optional) will contain totals. If no FIELDS {list} is present, all numeric type fields are totaled. Other type fields will contain the contents of the first record in that set.

---

* There is a 128 field limit in dBASE III, 32 field limit in dBASE II.

The TO {data file} will have the same structure as the data file from which the totals are drawn. If the file existed before, it will be replaced.*

This command is useful for creating summary information for input into a spreadsheet programs. For instance, if you had a data file PROPERTY.DBF of properties with fields for city, purchase price, and current market value, you could easily create a summary file with total purchase prices and market values by city:

```
use property
index on city to indxfile
total on city to sumfile
```

If your data file contained 150 records with information on properties in 5 different cities, SUMFILE.DBF would contain 5 records, each with the total purchase price and total market value of the properties in a specific city. The field CITY would contain the name of the city to which the totals pertained.

GUIDED ACTIVITY

This activity requires you to use the UPDATE command.

1. Follow the startup procedure for your version of dBASE as outlined in Unit 2.

2. Create a file named PRICECH with the following structure:

Field	Field name	Type	Width	Dec
1	FGID	Character	4	
2	NEW_PRICE	Numeric	6	2

3. Enter the following data into PRICECH.DBF

FGID	NEW_PRICE
1005	2.50
1002	2.50
1004	2.50
1003	2.50
1007	0.89
1009	0.51

---

* In dBASE II, if the TO {data file} existed before the command, then its structure will be unaltered and only those numeric fields which exist in the TO {data file} will be totaled. If the TO {data file} did not exist, then the file will be created with the same structure as the USE file (either all fields or for the FIELDS listed).

```
. use fin_good
. index on fgid to fin_good
fin_good.ndx already exists, overwrite it? (Y/N) Yes
      17 records indexed
. select b
. use pricech
. select a
. update on fgid from b replace sell_price with b->new_price random
      6 records updated
. _
```

FIGURE 17-1 Illustration of the UPDATE Command
Note: Items entered by user are in **boldface**

4. Update FIN_GOOD.DBF based on the information in PRICECH.DBF , as illustrated in Figure 17-1.

✔**CHECKPOINT**
What command do you use for the update?

_____

5. Do a screen print to show the commands used, and LIST TO PRINT to demonstrate that the command worked.

6. When you have completed all of the above, give the command QUIT to exit dBASE. Remember to backup your work. If everything is proper, turn off the computer and return the dBASE software to the Lab Supervisor.

REVIEW QUESTIONS

1. What is an update operation?

2. What is a join operation?

*3. If you were to use the TOTAL command on the RAW_MATL file, indexed by RMID, how many records would be in the file created by TOTAL? Why?

DOCUMENTATION RESEARCH

Using the reference manual, determine the answer to the following questions which deal with the commands discussed in this Unit. I recommend you also write the page number by the discussion of the command, above.

1. UPDATE ON {key} FROM {alias} REPLACE {field} WITH {expression} RANDOM -- what will happen if the {key} field is not unique in the target database?

2. JOIN WITH {alias} TO {file} FOR {condition} -- what is the minimum number of records in the target {file}? the maximum number of records?

3. TOTAL ON {key} TO {data file} -- what will appear in character, date, and logical type fields of the target data file?

Application

F

CHEZ JACQUES (III)

This application exercise requires you to use multiple file capabilities of dBASE. Although it can be accomplished in dBASE II, it is much better to attempt this application only if you have dBASE III.

1. Follow the startup procedure for your version of dBASE as outlined in Unit 2.

2. Write a command file named BOM.PRG which will compute a Bill of Materials for all items in the finished goods file. A sample Bill of Materials appears in Figure F-1. The Bill of Materials that you compute may have different numbers due to changes you have made in the finished goods and raw materials files.

   The Bill of Materials should

   a. print the finished item description and selling price,

   b. list all raw materials with description, quantity (in the finished product) and cost,

   c. compute and print the total cost of the raw materials in the item and the margin (price - cost).

   You have done much of the necessary work for items b. and c. in the guided activities with Units 15 and 16. Your program will need another loop to circulate through the finished goods file, with the loop through the mix file included within the finished goods loop. The basic structure of the program will therefore be:

```
Hamburger
-----------------------------------------------
all-beef patty   1      0.10
pickle slice     2      0.03
regular bun      1      0.10
catsup (oz.)     1      0.04
Selling Price         0.62
Total Cost              0.30
Margin                             0.32

Cheese Burger
-----------------------------------------------
all-beef patty   1      0.10
pickle slice     2      0.03
regular bun      1      0.10
catsup (oz.)     1      0.04
cheese slice     1      0.02
Selling Price         0.89
Total Cost              0.32
Margin                             0.57
```

FIGURE F-1 Portion of a Bill of Materials

```
set talk off
open all files, index and set relations as necessary
start loop through finished goods file
    start loop through mix file
        list and sum for raw material
        next record in mix file
    end of mix file loop
    next record in finished goods file
end of finished goods file loop
set talk on
```

I leave it to you to fill in the details.

3. Print a copy of your bill of materials. Do this by giving the command
    SET PRINT ON before you give the command DO BOM .

4. Print a copy of your command file.

5. When you have completed all of the above, exit dBASE. Remember to backup your work.
    If everything is proper, turn off the computer and return the dBASE software to the
    Lab Supervisor.

Appendix

A GETTING STARTED ON YOUR MICROCOMPUTER

Laura B. Ruff
Mary K. Weitzer
Steven C. Ross

This appendix covers the knowledge necessary to use application software with the IBM PC or compatible microcomputers along with the disk operating system (DOS). It is not intended to make you an expert in DOS, but rather to provide some level of competence by providing the necessary operations external to the software discussed in this manual.

PART I: THE KEYBOARD

The IBM and other personal computers have over 80 keys, about 40 more than most typewriters. An illustration of the keyboard appears inside the back cover. Many of the "extra" keys have symbols or mnemonics rather than characters. To minimize confusion, the following conventions are used in the **Understanding and Using** microcomputing series.

Keys with multiple character names will have those names spelled out, usually followed by the word "key." Examples include the F1 key, the Ins key, the Home key, and the Del key. Keys with symbols only will have the key name enclosed in < > signs:

<TAB>   gray key just below Esc key marked with two arrows

<SHIFT>   gray keys--one between Ctrl and Alt keys, the other just above Caps
                   Lock key, marked with hollow upward arrows

<BACKSPACE>   gray key in top row of keyboard with arrow pointing to the left

<CR>   gray key between <BACKSPACE> and PrtSc keys marked with bent arrow

<ARROW KEYS>   white keys on right of keyboard each marked with an arrow--also called
                   <UP>, <LEFT>, <DOWN>, and <RIGHT>--note that <LEFT> and
                   <BACKSPACE> are two different keys and that they do different things.

It is assumed that if a character is shown in upper case, or if the character is a symbol that requires the use of <SHIFT>, you will know that the <SHIFT> should be held down in order to get the desired character.

FUNCTION KEYS

These ten keys are located in two rows along the left edge of the keyboard. Most application software packages make special use of these keys. Although these keys also have special meanings when used by DOS, we will ignore those uses here to avoid confusion with the application program which is the subject of this book.

MULTIPLE KEY COMBINATIONS

On a typewriter, the <SHIFT> is used in conjunction with a letter key in order to produce a capital letter. The same is true on a computer. On a computer, the Ctrl and Alt keys act as modifying keys, so that if either of those keys is used in conjunction with another key, the original letter is modified. These keys are manipulated in the same manner as the <SHIFT> key. For example, to type Alt + M, hold down the Alt key and press M.

WHAT IS "TOGGLE"

Toggle keys act as on-off switches. Press them once and they are activated; press them a second time and they are deactivated. Examples of toggle keys include the Num Lock key (activates the numeric key pad), the Ctrl + PrtSc combination (prints the current screen when in DOS), and the Caps Lock key.

CAPS LOCK KEY

The Caps Lock key shifts all alphabet (A...Z) keys to upper case, yet has no effect on any key which does not contain a letter of the alphabet. This is unlike a typewriter, where the shift lock locks all keys into shifted characters. The Caps Lock key is a toggle key.

NUMERIC KEYPAD KEYS

These are the keys on the right side of the keyboard which are configured as a 10-key pad. The keys with arrows on them are referred to as <ARROW KEYS> or as <UP>, <LEFT>, <DOWN>, and <RIGHT>. The other keypad keys are referred to by the text which appears on the key: Home, PgUp, PgDn, End, Del, and Ins. The numeric function of the keys can be activated by using the Num Lock key (a toggle key). Most of the keys have no effect when in DOS, but are used by many application programs to control movement on the screen.

PART II: GETTING STARTED

LOADING DOS

Loading DOS means that some of the DOS programs are read from the DOS disk into the computer's memory. You must load DOS before you can use any application software or any of the system's utilities.

Some application software will require you to use the DOS disk to load the system before loading the application program. Other application software will give you instructions on how to install DOS onto the software program disk in order to make it self-loading and to give the user some system capabilities without having to switch disks.

DOS PROMPT

The DOS or system prompt (A> with a single or dual drive system or C> with a hard disk) tells you that it is your turn to type information; that is, you must tell DOS what to do by entering a command.

The system prompt's letter also indicates the default drive. The default drive is the disk drive that DOS will go to automatically if you do not type a drive specification. On a single or dual drive system, the default drive is usually A>, while on a hard disk system, the default drive will usually be C>. Simply typing the drive letter will override the default. If you intend to perform a number of operations on the files in the drive which is not the default, you may wish to change the default disk drive. In the **Understanding and Using Series**, all drive specifications are indicated.

START-UP PROCEDURES
IF MICROCOMPUTER SYSTEM IS TURNED OFF

Single or Dual Disk Drives

1. The door on Disk Drive A should be open. Insert the DOS disk or a program disk on which DOS has been installed.

2. When the disk is fully inserted, close the drive door.

3. If you have dual disk drives and have a second disk for data, insert it in Disk Drive B.

4. When the disk is fully inserted, close the drive door.

5. Make sure that the printer is turned on and that the power, ready, and online lights (or their equivalent) are on.

6. Turn on the power switch.

7. When the red in-use disk drive lights go off, the program should be loaded.

8. Adjust the contrast controls on the monitor to a comfortable level.

9. If you have a single disk drive and a data disk, remove the program disk from Drive A.

10. Insert the data disk into Drive A.

11. When the disk is fully inserted, close the drive door.

Hard Disk

1. Make sure that the printer is turned on and that the power, ready, and online lights (or their equivalent) are on.

2. Turn on the power switch.

3. When the red in-use disk drive lights go off, the program should be loaded.

4. Adjust the contrast controls on the monitor to a comfortable level.

5. After the program has loaded, you may insert a data disk in Drive A.

START-UP PROCEDURES
IF MICROCOMPUTER SYSTEM IS TURNED ON

Single or Dual Drive System

1. Adjust the contrast controls on the monitor.

2. The door on Disk Drive A should be open. Insert the DOS disk or a program which has been set up with DOS.

3. When the disk is fully inserted, close the drive door.

4. If you have a second disk for data, insert it in Disk Drive B.

5. When the disk is fully inserted, close the drive door.

6. Make sure that the printer is turned on and that the power, ready, and online lights (or their equivalent) are on.

7. Load the program by pressing and holding the Ctrl key + the Alt key. Then, press the Del Key. RELEASE ALL THREE KEYS.

8. When the red in-use disk drive lights go off, the program should be loaded. Continue with the procedures related to the program being used.

Hard Disk System

1. Make sure that the printer is turned on and that the power, ready, and online lights (or their equivalent) are on.

2. Load the program. Press and hold the Ctrl key + the Alt Key. Then, touch the Del Key. RELEASE ALL THREE KEYS.

3. When the red in-use disk drive lights go off, the program should be loaded.

4. Adjust the contrast controls on the monitor.

5. After the program has loaded, you may insert a data disk in Drive A.

6. Continue with the procedures related to the program being used.

SETTING THE DATE AND TIME

It is strongly recommended that you allow the system to "time stamp" the files you are using by setting the date and time whenever you begin a work session. (Some microcomputers may have special boards with clocks that will automatically set the time. If your system has this feature, you may skip these procedures.)

1. When DOS asks for the current date, type today's date using the following format: xx/xx/xx   OR xx-xx-xx . Fill in appropriate numbers where x's appear. Do not type the name of the day. This will result in an "invalid date" prompt. (For example: April 30, 1986 is entered as 4-30-86 or 4/30/86.)

2. Press <CR>

3. When DOS asks for the time, type the current time using this format: xx:xx . Fill in appropriate numbers where x's appear using 24-hour time to distinguish a.m. from p.m. Do not type "a.m." or "p.m." (For example, 10:15 a.m. is simply typed as 10:15 -- no other time indicators are required. If you were starting at 1:15 in the afternoon, you would type 13:15.)

4. Press <CR>

   The DOS prompt will appear on the screen (A> with a single or dual drive system or C> with a hard disk).

Resetting the date

If you entered the wrong date or forgot to enter the date at system start up or reset, you may reset the date with the Date command:

1. Type **DATE**

2. Press **<CR>**

3. Then type in the appropriate date according to the format discussed earlier.

Resetting the time

If you entered the wrong time or forgot to enter the time at system start up or reset, you may reset the time with the TIME command:

1. Type **TIME**.

2. Press **<CR>**

3. Then type in the appropriate time according to the format discussed earlier.

SHUT-DOWN PROCEDURES

1. Make sure that you have followed the proper escape or exit procedures for the software program you are using. Failure to follow such precautions may result in lost data.

2. When the red in-use disk drive lights are off for both drives, remove the disk from one of the drives. Do not close the drive door.

3. Follow the same procedure and remove the disk from the other drive. Do not close the drive door.

4. If you know that you or someone else will be using the system within a short amount of time, it is advisable to leave the system turned on in order to minimize wear and tear. However, in order to protect your display, turn down the contrast control button.

PART III: ISSUING COMMANDS

TO ISSUE COMMANDS

1. The command must be typed exactly as described in this appendix, including any spaces within the command.

2. Commands may be typed in upper-case or lower-case. DOS will read them as upper-case.

3. If the command you type contains a typographical error, a missing space, or an extra space the prompt "Bad Command or File Name" will appear after you press <CR>. If this prompt does appear, simply retype the command correctly.

4. Be sure to press <CR> after you have typed in any command in order to tell the system to begin the procedure.

TO CORRECT A TYPING MISTAKE BEFORE YOU TOUCH <CR>

1. The <BACKSPACE> key may be used to correct errors made while in DOS. Characters will be erased as you backspace. The <LEFT ARROW> will also move the cursor to the left, however, characters will not be erased as the cursor moves to the left.

2. If a line has many errors, just touch the Esc key. A backslash (\) will appear. The cursor will move down one line on the screen, and even though the error-filled line(s) still appear on the screen, it is deleted from memory. The system then waits for your corrected command.

TO STOP A COMMAND IN PROGRESS

1. Hold down the **Ctrl Key** + the **Break Key**.

   This key has Scroll Lock on the top and Break on the forward edge.

2. Release both keys. Execution of the command will halt.

3. The system command (A> or C>) will reappear and you can type your next command.

PARAMETERS

Parameters are items that can be included in DOS command statements in order to specify additional information to the system. Some parameters are required, others are optional. If you do not include some parameters, a default value will be provided by the system. Examples of some of the parameters you will be working with frequently when using DOS follow.

Parameter	Explanation
[filespec]	A filespec will appear as [d:][filename][.ext]
	Example: B:myfile.doc
	A:yourfile
	anyfiles.bas
	thisfile

An explanation of each part of the filespec follows.

[d:]   This parameter is the drive indicator. You enter the drive letter
                            followed by a colon to indicate the intended drive.

                            For example when you do a directory of the disk in Drive B (when B
                            is not the default drive), you will type **DIR B:** After you
                            press <CR>, the system will display the directory of the disk in
                            drive B.

                            If you do not specify a drive in the command, the system will
                            assume the default drive is intended. For example, if the default
                            drive is Drive A, you type **DIR**. When you press the <CR> key,
                            the system will give you a directory of the disk in Drive A.

[filename]   You may assign any name to a file as long as it meets the following
                            criteria. The name assigned to the file can have from 1 to 8
                            characters. The only valid characters are: A-Z 0-9 $ & @ % /
                            \ _ - () " {} # !

                            The filename parameters are in force even when you are using
                            application software, but some software will not accept all of the
                            characters listed above.

[.ext]   You may assign an optional filename extension with from 1 to 3
                            characters. If you specify the optional 3-character extension, it
                            must be separated from the filename by a period. Sometimes you
                            cannot specify the filename extension because the application
                            program does so automatically.

                            Again, the above characters are the only valid characters.
                            If an extension is assigned, you must include it as part of the
                            filespec whenever you want the system to locate the file.

CHANGE DEFAULT DRIVE

Change the Default Drive to B>

 1. Type **B:**

 2. Press <CR>

Change the Default Drive to A>

 1. Type **A:**

 2. Press <CR>

Change the default drive to C>

1. Type **C:**

2. Press **<CR>**

The last command will not work unless you have a hard disk drive or some other special configuration.

CHECKDISK

The Checkdisk command produces a disk and memory status report. The report will tell you how much space your files are using on the disk, how much space is still available on the disk, and whether the disk has any bad sectors (if a disk does have bad sectors, you might want to use the COPY *.* command to copy all your files to another formatted disk). Checkdisk will also indicate how much memory is available in the system unit you are using.

1. The DOS disk should be in the default drive (either A> or C>) and the disk to be checked should be in Drive B (single or dual drive system) or Drive C (hard disk).

2. Type **CHKDSK B: or CHKDSK A: or CHKDSK C:**

3. Press **<CR>**

COPY

The copy command allows you to transfer a copy of a file(s) from one disk to another without erasing any of the data located on the disk to which you are copying. This is one method that may be used to backup your data disks.

The disk that contains the file(s) you wish to copy is called the source disk. The disk to which you are copying the files is called the target or destination disk.

In order to use this command, the target disk must already have been formatted. The name of the file to be copied must be spelled correctly and include the complete filespec (drive designation [if not default drive], file name, and any optional extension).

1. DOS must be loaded.

2. Place the source disk in one of the drives and the target disk in the other drive.

3. Type **COPY**, enter the source drive and filename next, and then enter the target drive.The command is terminated by <CR>.

a. If the file you wish to copy is in Drive A and the target disk is in Drive B, you would type the command as follows:

COPY A:FILENAME.EXT B:

Since a new filename is not specified, DOS will assume you want the filename to stay the same.

b. If the file you wish to copy is in Drive B and the target disk is in Drive A, you would type the command as follows:

COPY B:FILENAME.EXT A:

Since a new filename is not specified, DOS will assume you want the filename to stay the same.

c. If the file you wish to copy is in Drive C (root directory) and the target disk is in Drive A, you would type the command as follows:

COPY C:FILENAME.EXT A:

Since a new filename is specified, DOS will assume you want the filename to stay the same.

With any form of the command, you are specifying that you want to copy the named file from the first drive designated in the command to the disk located in the second drive indicated in the command.

4. If the system cannot find the file, it will indicate "0 Files copied." Check the spelling of the filename. Be sure you have included an extension if an extension was assigned to the file. If you made a mistake in typing the command, just retype it at the DOS prompt as described previously.

COPY USING GLOBAL CHARACTER (*)

When you wish to copy more than one file and there is some common element in the names of the files you wish to copy, you can use the global character (*) to expedite the process.

1. DOS should be loaded.

2. Remove the DOS disk from Drive A.

3. Insert the source disk and/or the target disk in the disk drives.

a. If the source disk is in Drive A and the target disk is in Drive B and the files you wish to copy have the extension in common, type:

COPY A:*.EXT B:

Press <CR>

Since a new filename is not specified, DOS will assume you want the filename to stay the same.

b. If the source disk is in Drive B and the target disk is in Drive A and the files you wish to copy have the extension in common, type:

COPY B:*.EXT A:

Press **<CR>**

Since a new filename is not specified, DOS will assume you want the filename to stay the same.

c. If the source disk is in Drive C (root directory) and the target disk is in Drive A and the files you wish to copy have the extension in common, type:

COPY C:*.EXT A:

Press **<CR>**

Since a new filename is not specified, DOS will assume you want the filename to stay the same.

d. If the source disk is in Drive A and the target disk is in Drive B and the files you wish to copy have the filename in common, type:

COPY A:FILENAME.* B:

Press **<CR>**

e. If the source disk is in Drive B and the target disk is in Drive A and the files you wish to copy have the filename in common, type:

COPY B:FILENAME.* A:

Press **<CR>**

f. If the source disk is in Drive C (root directory) and the target disk is in Drive A and the files you wish to copy have the filename in common, type:

COPY C:FILENAME.* A:

Press **<CR>**

4. If the system cannot find the files, it will indicate "0 Files copied." Check the spelling of the filename. Be sure you have included an extension if an extension was assigned to the file. If you made a mistake in typing the command, just retype it at the DOS prompt as described previously.

COPY *.* (File-by-file)

This command will copy the entire contents of the source disk onto a <u>formatted</u> target disk without erasing any data that may be on the target disk.

1. DOS must be loaded.

2. Remove the DOS disk from Drive A.

3. Insert the source disk and the target disk in the drives.

   a. If the source disk is in Drive A and the target disk is in Drive B, type:

   COPY A:*.* B:

   Press <CR>

   b. If the source disk is in Drive B and the target disk is in Drive A, type:

   COPY B:*.* A:

   Press <CR>

   c. If the source disk is in Drive A and the target disk is Drive C, type:

   COPY A:*.* C:

4. When the copy is complete, the number of files copied will appear on the screen (or you will receive the message that there is insufficient disk space).

DELETE (ERASE FILE)

This command is used to delete a specified file from a disk in the designated drive.

1. DOS must be loaded but the DOS disk does not have to be in the drive when the command is given.

2. Make sure the disk containing the file to be deleted is in the drive before you press <CR>.

   a. If the disk containing the file(s) to be deleted is in Drive B, type:

   DEL B:FILENAME.EXT or ERASE B:FILENAME.EXT

   Press <CR>

b. If the disk containing the file(s) to be deleted is in Drive A, type:

DEL A:FILENAME.EXT or ERASE A:FILENAME.EXT

Press **<CR>**

c. If the file(s) to be deleted is in Drive C, type:

DEL C:FILENAME.EXT or ERASE C:FILENAME.EXT

Press **<CR>**

3. If the file is successfully erased, there will be no message. The global character can be used with the Delete (or Erase) command just as it was used with the copy command. However, the file-by-file delete is not recommended. Formatting is the preferred method of erasing all of the files off a floppy disk.

4. If the system cannot find the file, it will give you an error message. Check the spelling of the filename. Be sure you have included an extension if an extension was assigned to the file. If you made a mistake in typing the command, just retype it at the DOS prompt.

DIRECTORY

The directory is a listing of all the files located on the disk in the specified drive. It is possible to display a directory on a disk in any drive on the system.

1. DOS must be loaded.

a. If you wish to see a directory on the disk in Drive B, type:

DIR B:

Press **<CR>**

b. If you wish to see a directory on the disk in Drive A, type:

DIR A:

Press **<CR>**

c. If you wish to see a directory of the disk in Drive C, type:

Dir C:

2. Press **<CR>**

3. A listing of the names of the files located on the disk in the designated drive will appear.

DIRECTORY (PAUSE)

With this form of the directory command the listing pauses so that you can read the first lines of the directory. When you are ready, press any key to continue the listing.

1. Type **DIR/P A: or DIR/P B: or DIR/P C:**

2. Press **<CR>**

DIRECTORY (WIDE)

This form of the directory command produces a wide display of the directory, which lists only the file names.

1. Type **DIR/W A: or DIR/W B: or DIR/W C:**

2. Press **<CR>**

DIRECTORY (PRINT)

If you would like to print the directory rather than have it appear on screen, use the following command.

1. Type **DIR A:>PRN or DIR B:>PRN or DIR C:>PRN**

2. Press **<CR>**

The directory will print.

DISKCOPY

The diskcopy command will copy the entire contents of a disk onto another disk. The diskcopy command will format the target disk if necessary. Be careful when you use the diskcopy command because any files on the target disk will be erased.

1. Type **DISKCOPY A: B: or DISKCOPY B: A:**

2. Press **<CR>**

TO STOP THE SCREEN FROM SCROLLING

If information appears on the screen and then scrolls off before you can read it, as frequently happens when you display a long directory, the following procedure will stop the scrolling until you are ready for it to continue.

1. Press the **Ctrl Key** + the **Num Lock Key**.

2. Then, release both keys. The scrolling will stop.

3. Press any key to restart the scrolling.

FORMAT

The format command can be used to format a blank disk (a disk cannot be used on the system until it is formatted) or to erase an entire disk that contains data you no longer need. The disk can then be reused. Unless you wish to use the format command to erase a disk, you will have to format each disk only once.

CAUTION: This command will erase the entire contents of disk. If you have any doubts about the contents of the disk you are going to format, display a directory of the disk to make sure that it does not contain any files you want to keep (see DIRECTORY in this appendix).

1. DOS should be loaded and the DOS disk should be in Drive A.

2. Type **Format B:**

3. Press **<CR>**

4. When the system prompts you to insert a new disk in the designated drive, make sure that the disk you wish to format is in the designated drive.

5. Touch any key to begin the formatting process.

6. When the formatting process is complete, you will be asked if you wish to format another disk. If you wish to format another disk, type the letter "Y" for "yes" and follow the screen prompts to insert a blank disk. If you do not wish to format another disk, type the letter "N" for "no." Your data disk is now ready to be used with the system.

FORMAT WITH VOLUME LABEL

By using the V option of the format command you put an electronic label on your disk. When you use the DIR or CHKDSK commands, this electronic volume label will be displayed.

1. DOS should be loaded and the DOS disk should be in Drive A. A blank disk should be in drive B.

2. Type **FORMAT B:/V**

3. Press **<CR>**

4. When the system prompts you to insert a new disk in the designated drive, make sure that the disk you wish to format is in the designated drive.

5. Touch any key to begin the formatting process.

6. Part of the process will be completed when the following appears on the screen:

Formatting. . .Format complete

Volume label (11 characters, ENTER for none)?

7. Type in the label you want to use, for example your name, social security number, or the disk number. Review the filename parameters for a list of illegal characters.

8. Press <CR>

9. When the formatting process is complete, you will be asked if you wish to format another disk. If you wish to format another disk, type the letter "Y" for "yes" and follow the screen prompts to insert a blank disk. If you do not wish to format another disk, type the letter "N" for "no." Your data disk is now ready to be used with the system.

PRINT SCREEN FUNCTION

The print screen function is available through DOS. It allows you to print an exact copy of what appears on the screen.

1. Be sure DOS is loaded and that the printer is turned on and online.

2. Press and hold <SHIFT> + PrtSc Key.

3. Release both keys. The contents of the screen will print.

OUTPUT TO PRINTER FUNCTION

When the output to printer or echo function is activated, anything that is typed on the keyboard will appear on both the screen and on paper.

1. Be sure DOS is loaded.

2. Make sure that the printer is turned on and online.

3. Press and hold the Ctrl Key and then just touch the PrtSc Key. When you use these keys to activate the output to printer, it will appear that nothing has happened.

4. Release both keys.

5. In order to see if the function has been activated, press the **<CR>** key a few times. The paper will advance one line and print the command prompt (e.g. A>) each time you press <CR>.

6. If you do not get any printer response, repeat the procedure.

HOW TO DEACTIVATE OUTPUT TO PRINTER

Until you deactivate the output to printer, everything that appears on the display will also appear on paper.

1. Make sure the printer is online. Press and hold the **Ctrl Key** and then just <u>touch</u> the **PrtSc Key**.

2. Release both keys.

3. This will stop the output to the printer. In order to check to be sure that the function is no longer active, press the **<CR>** key a few times. If the paper does not advance one line and print the command prompt each time you press <CR>, the output to printer function is deactivated.

4. If you do get a printer response, repeat the procedure.

Appendix

B ANSWERS TO CHECK-POINT QUESTIONS

ANSWERS TO ✔CHECKPOINT

p. 34
  # 3-12a. remove the dBASE disk from the A drive
  # 3-12b. copy b:*.* a:
pp. 52-53
  # 4-3. list to print for cost<0.10
  # 4-4. list to print for cost*inventory>10
  # 4-5. list to print for '(oz.)'$desc
  # 4-6. set heading off; list off for cost*inventory>50
p. 58
  # 5-2a. use fin__good
  # 5-2c. use raw__matl
p. 70
  # 6-5. the 8 oz. cup record (number 5) because it has the lowest RMID
pp. 84-85
  # 7-5. set function 10 to 'DIR *.*;'
  # 7-8. copy to raw2
  # 7-9. copy to merge.txt delimited
p. 96
  # 8-3. replace all cost with cost*1.2
  # 8-4. change for 'cup'$desc
  # 8-5a. delete for inventory>=100
  # 8-5b. set deleted off; recall all
p. 116
  # 9-7. index on rmid to temp; report form raw__matl to print
p. 125
  #10-7. index on rmid to temp; label form raw__matl to print
p. 138
  #11-3. sum cost*inventory to sum
  #11-4. sum inventory to count
  #11-5. ? sum/count

pp. 157-58
  #13-2a. use fin__good
  #13-2b. do while .not. eof( )
  #13-2c. display desc,sell__price
  #13-2d. input 'New Price ' to new__price
  #13-2e. replace sell__price with new__price
  #13-2f. skip
  #13-2g. enddo
p. 165
  #14-2a. use fin__good
  #14-2b. do while .not. eof( )
  #14-2c. clear
  #14-2d. @ 5,5 say desc
  #14-2e. @ 7,5 get sell__price
        read
  #14-2f. skip
  #14-2g. enddo
pp. 177-78
  #15-2a. use mix
  #15-2b. index on fgid to mix
  #15-2c. select 2 (dBASE III) *or* select secondary (dBASE II)
  #15-2d. use raw__matl
  #15-2e. index on rmid to raw__matl
  #15-2f. select 1 *or* select primary
  #15-2g. totcost=0 (dBASE III only) *or* store 0 to totcost
  #15-2h. accept 'Enter FGID ' to m__fgid (dBASE III)
        or accept 'Enter FGID ' to m:fgid (dBASE II)
  #15-2i. seek m__fgid *or* find &m__fgid (dBASE III)
        or find &m:fgid (dBASE II)
  #15-2j. do while fgid=m__fgid (dBASE III) *or* do while fgid=m:fgid (dBASE II)
  #15-2k. select 2 *or* select secondary
  #15-2l. seek a->rmid (dBASE III) *or* find &p.rmid (dBASE II)
  #15-2m. select 1 *or* select primary
  #15-2n. totcost=totcost+a->rm__qty*b->cost (dBASE III)
        or store p.rm:qty*s.cost+totcost to totcost (dBASE II)
  #15-2o. skip
  #15-2p. enddo
  #15-2q. ? totcost
pp. 185-86
  #16-2a. use mix
  #16-2b. index on fgid to mix
  #16-2c. select 2
  #16-2d. use raw__matl
  #16-2e. index on rmid to raw__matl
  #16-2f. select 1
  #16-2g. set relation to rmid into b
  #16-2h. totcost=0
  #16-2i. accept 'Enter FGID ' to m__fgid
  #16-2j. seek m__fgid *or* find &m__fgid
  #16-2k. do while fgid=m__fgid
  #16-2l. totcost=totcost+a->rm__qty*b->cost

#16-2m. skip
#16-2n. enddo
#16-2o. ? totcost
p. 192
#17-4. assuming that you have opened the proper files and that pricech.dbf
is in the second (b) work area ...
update on fgid from b replace sell_price with b->new_price random

ANSWERS TO SELECTED REVIEW QUESTIONS

pp. 8-9
1-4. in dBASE II: 32; in dBASE III: 128
1-5a. 4 bytes
1-5c. 4 bytes
1-5d. 3 bytes minimum, 4 bytes recommended so quantity can exceed 999
p. 19
2-2a. invokes help menus
2-2e. moves to previous record or screen display
2-2f. deletes the character at the cursor
2-2g. exit and save from most editing situations
pp. 34-35
3-2a. TICKER, Char/text,4 (other names are possible, and greater width)
3-2b. PRICE, Numeric,7,3
3-2c. PHONE, Char/text,13
3-2d. SMOKER, Logical (width of 1 is automatic)
3-2e. DATE, Date (width of 8 is automatic)
pp. 53-54
4-2. the order in which the operations in conditions and expressions are performed
4-4a. False (capitalization is different)
4-4b. False
4-4c. True
4-4d. True
4-4f. True (age>size is False and .not. False is True)
4-4g. False (first condition is False -- both must be True with .and.)
4-4h. True (one of the conditions is True)
4-4j. False (age = 25)
4-5. list to print for (cost*inventory > 50)
4-6. the $ must be used when the comparison does not start with the first character
pp. 58-59
5-1. use fin_good ; count for (sell_price<1)
5-3. use raw_matl ; sum cost*inventory
5-5. sum cost*inventory for (.not.('(oz.)'$desc))
p. 71
6-3. use raw_matl ; index on rmid to raw_matl
6-4b. the order in which the data reside on the disk
6-4c. the order in which the data appear to be based on the index key
6-5a. find 0010
6-6a. the dot prompt without any "No Find" message
6-6b. dBASE will display the message "No Find"
6-6c. dBASE displays the message "Record = n" where n is a record number

6-6d. dBASE displays the message "End of File"

6-7. use fin_good ; index on sell_price to temp ; list

6-9. use locate when you wish to process the records, list when viewing is sufficient.

p. 85

7-3. display status

7-6. use raw_matl ; copy to textfile fields desc, cost delimited

p. 97

8-2a. replace all age with age+1

8-2b. change fields name, phone for 'Marketing'$department

8-2c. locate for (Smith$last_name) ; edit

p. 116

9-2. use raw_matl index raw_matl ; report form raw_matl

p. 138

11-1. a field is part of a data base, a variable is in memory

11-3a. store 'Genghis Khan' to name   or   name = 'Genghis Khan' (dBASE III)

11-3b. store 16 to age   or   age = 16

11-4a. store name+'the Magnificent' to name or name=name+'the Magnificent'

11-4b. store age*2 to older   or   older = age*2

11-6. save to memory

11-7. restore from memory additive

p. 150

12-2. another name for command file

12-3. a series of repeated instructions

12-4. modify command {filename}

12-6. do {filename}

pp. 158-59

13-2a. go 15

13-2b. skip

13-2c. find New York

13-3a. accept 'Name: ' to m_name

13-3b. input 'Age: ' to m_age

13-4. ? m_name ; ? m_age

13-5. append blank

13-6. replace

p. 166

14-2. 0,79

p. 179

15-4a. ? b->red+a->cleveland (dBASE III)   ? s.red+p.cleveland (dBASE II)

15-4b. ? b->red - b->white (dBASE III)   ? s.red - s.white (dBASE II)

15-5. in dBASE II: select secondary ; replace red with 200

      in dBASE III: select b ; replace red with 200

p. 187

16-1. a link between two data files

p. 193

17-3. 19 records because each RMID is different

INDEX

SYMBOLS INDEX

!
!(char string), 49

#
#, 47, 143, 152, 153

$
$, 46, 47, 102
$(char expression,start,length), 49

&
&, 48, 137, 152, 171

'
'...', 46

(
( ), 45

*
*, 45, 82, 90, 145
**, 45
DEL, 91

+
+, 45, 46, 122

-
-, 45
->, 133, 175

.
"...", 46
.AND., 47
.NOT., 47
.OR., 47

/
/, 45

<
<, 47
<=, 47
<>, 47

=
=, 47, 134

>
>, 47
>=, 47

?
?, 82, 155
??, 155

@
@, 162, 163
@ GET, 163
@ SAY, 162
@(char string 1,char string 2), 48

[
[...], 46

^
^, 45

{
{ }, 22

TOPICAL INDEX

1
1:1 relation, 182
1:M relation, 182

A
ACCEPT, 133, 154
Ad hoc inquiry, 65
Addition, 45
ADDITIVE, 135
ALIAS, 175
  with SET RELATION command, 183
APPEND, 27, 38, 64, 80
APPEND BLANK, 156
APPEND FROM, 95
APPEND FROM {filename} DELIMITED, 83
APPEND FROM {filename} SDF, 83
ASC(char string), 51
ASCII collating sequence, 62
ASCII text, 82
AT(char string 1,char string 2), 48
AVERAGE, 56, 133, 134

B
Beginning of file function, 142
binary +,-, 45
BOF( ), 142
Break, 15
BROWSE, 88, 90
Byte, 4

C
Calculator command, 44
CANCEL, 146, 148
Capacity Considerations, 6
CASE, 147
CDOW(date variable), 50
CHANGE, 88, 89
Change field type, 94
Character day of week function, 50
Character month function, 50
Character string, 25
Character to date function, 50
CHR(numeric expression), 48
CLEAR, 145, 155, 164
CLEAR ALL, 145, 174
CMONTH(date variable), 50
COBOL, 82
COL( ), 51
Command parameters, 22

Command verb, 22
Comment, 145
Computed expressions vs. logical
  conditions, 44
Concatenation, 46, 122
CONFIG.DB, 77, 79
CONFIG.SYS, 12
Constraints, 6
CONTINUE, 68, 153
COPY, 80, 81
COPY FILE, 81
COPY TO, 95
COPY TO {filename} DELIMITED, 82
COUNT, 55, 102, 133, 134
CREATE, 23, 38, 80, 84, 94
CREATE LABEL, 121
CREATE REPORT, 107
CTOD(char expression), 50
Current record, 66
Current record function, 143

D
Data Base, 3
Data Base Management System, 3, 181
Data Dictionary, 4
Data File, 6
Date, 25
Date function, 50
Date to character function, 50, 122
DATE( ), 50
DAY(date variable), 51
dBASE
  starting, 15
DBF, 4, 23, 80, 182
DBMS, 3, 181
DBT, 80
Debugging, 157
Decimal places, 26
DELETE, 91, 103
Delete a field, 94
DELETE FILE, 82
DELETE FOR, 91
DELETE RECORD, 91
Deleted record, 90
Deleted records, 90
DELETED( ), 90
Deleting files, 82
DELIMITED, 82, 83
Design of Data Base System, 7

DIR, 81
Disk Operating System Disk
  special for dBASE III, 12
DISPLAY, 29, 51, 66, 73, 185
DISPLAY ALL, 29, 39
DISPLAY FILES, 81
DISPLAY FOR, 29, 47
DISPLAY MEMORY, 135
DISPLAY NEXT, 29, 68
DISPLAY STATUS, 76, 84
DISPLAY STRUCTURE, 38, 94, 95
Division, 45
DO, 144
DO CASE, 147
DO WHILE, 145
Dot prompt, 22
DOW(date variable), 51
DTOC(date expression), 50, 122

E
EDIT, 30, 39, 64, 88
EJECT, 155
ELSE, 147
End of file function, 143
ENDCASE, 147
ENDDO, 145
ENDIF, 147
Endless loop, 145
ENDTEXT, 155
EOF, 143, 153
EOF( ), 143, 146, 152, 153
Equal to, 47
ERASE, 82, 155
Error trapping routine, 170
Esc, 13
EXIT, 146
Exit to Operating System, 22
EXP(numeric expression), 49
Exponential function, 49
Exponentiation, 45
Extension to filename, 80

F
F1, 13, 108
F2, 13
F3, 30
F4, 82
F5, 27, 94
F6, 76
F7, 135
F8, 29

F9, 27
F10, 31
Field, 4, 5
  character, 25
  date, 25
  logical, 25
  memo, 25
  numeric, 25
Field contents, 109
Field header, 110
Field name, 132
  with alias, 175
Field Names, 5
Field specifications, 26
Fields, 132
File, 4
File extension, 80
File function, 143
FILE(string expression), 143
FIND, 66, 73, 152, 176
Flag character, 90
FMT, 80, 165
Form feed, 155
FORTRAN, 82
FRM, 80, 107, 112

G
GO, 153
GO BOTTOM, 66, 153
GO RECORD, 153
GO TOP, 66, 153
GOTO, 153, 174
GOTO RECORD, 153
Greater than, 47
Greater than or equal to, 47
Group subtotals, 109
Grouped, 105

H
Home the cursor, 155

I
IF, 147
Index, 4, 63, 73, 80, 91, 182
  updating, 64
Index key, 63
Index/sort, 64
Indexing
  benefits, 65
INPUT, 133, 153
INSERT, 28

Insert a field, 94
INSERT BEFORE, 28
INSERT mode, 15
INT(numeric expression), 49
Integer function, 49

J
JOIN, 190

K
Key, 4, 6, 63, 105, 181
Key expression, 63
Key expressions, 182

L
LABEL, 121
LABEL FORM, 123
Label format file, 121
Labels, 119
LBL, 80, 121, 123
LEN(char string), 48
Length function, 48
Less than, 47
Less than or equal to, 47
Link file, 183
LIST, 30, 39, 51, 65, 103, 185
LIST FILES, 81
LIST OFF, 51
LIST STATUS, 76
LIST TO PRINT, 30
LOCATE, 153
LOCATE FOR, 68
LOCATE NEXT, 69
Log function, 49
LOG(numeric expression), 49
Logical, 25
Logical comparison of character type
  data, 47
Logical conditions vs. computed
  expressions, 44
Logical record, 66
Loop, 145, 146
Lotus 1-2-3, 83
Lower case function, 49
LOWER(char string), 49

M
Macro function, 48, 137, 152
MailMerge, 83
Many to many relation, 182
MEM, 80, 135

Memo, 25
Memory variable, 132
Memory variable name, 132
Memory variable type, 132
MODIFY COMMAND, 143
MODIFY LABEL, 121
MODIFY REPORT, 107, 185
MODIFY STRUCTURE, 94, 95
MONTH(date variable), 51
Multiple indexes, 64
Multiplication, 45

N
N:M relation, 182
Name, 24
NDX, 4, 63, 80
No find, 67, 152
NOEJECT, 113
Not equal to, 47
NOTE, 145
Number to character function, 48
Numeric, 25
numeric accuracy, 25

O
OFF, 51
One to many relation, 182
One to one relation, 182
OTHERWISE, 147

P
PACK, 92
PARAMETERS, 133, 145
Pause, 154
PCOL( ), 51
Physical record, 66
PICTURE, 162, 164
Pointer
  record, 66
Pointers, 4
PRG, 80, 143, 144
PRIVATE, 145
PRN, 83
PROCEDURE, 145
Procedure file, 145
Prompt, 153
PROW( ), 51
PrtSc, 15
PUBLIC, 145

Q
QUIT, 22, 148

R
RANDOM, 190
Range checking, 164
RANK(char string), 51
READ, 163
RECALL, 91
RECALL FOR, 92
RECALL RECORD, 92
RECNO( ), 143, 153
Record, 4, 6
Record number, 132, 143
Record pointer, 66, 66
REINDEX, 64, 91
Relation, 182
   many to many, 182
   one to many, 182
   one to one, 182
Relational data base, 181
RELEASE, 135
RELEASE ALL, 135
RENAME, 82
REPLACE, 64, 88, 103, 156, 174
REPLACE ALL, 89
Report, 105
Report body, 105
Report column, 106
Report field, 106
REPORT FORM, 112, 113, 185
Report format file, 108
Report heading, 105
RESTORE, 164
RESTORE FROM, 135
RETURN, 144, 146, 148
ROUND(numeric expression,decimal), 49
Rounding function, 49
ROW( ), 51

S
Safety, 65
SAMPLE, 123
Sample Programs and Utilities Disk, 12
SAVE TO, 135
Saving Files
   QUIT command, 22, 28
   USE command, 27, 28
Screen print, 15
SDF, 82, 83, 84
SEEK, 153, 176

SELECT, 174
SET, 76
SET DEBUG ON, 157
SET DEFAULT, 77
SET DELETED, 91, 103
SET DEVICE TO PRINT, 163
SET DEVICE TO SCREEN, 163
SET ECHO ON, 157
SET FORMAT TO, 165
SET FUNCTION, 79
SET HEADING, 51
SET PRINT, 79
SET PRINT ON, 155
SET PROCEDURE, 145
SET RELATION, 174
SET RELATION TO, 183
SET STEP ON, 157
SET TALK ON, 157
SKIP, 146, 152, 174
SORT, 62
SPACE(number), 51
SQRT(numeric expression), 49
Square root function, 49
STORE, 133, 134, 164
STR(numeric expression,length,decimals),
   49, 122
String, 46
String function, 49, 122
String to numeric function, 50
Sub-totals, 105
SUBSTR(char expression,start,length), 49
Substring comparison, 46, 102
Substring function, 49
Substring search function, 48
Subtotal, 109
Subtraction, 45
SUM, 56, 133, 134
System Disk
   dBASE II, 12
   dBASE III, 11, 12

T
Table, 4
Tables, 181
TEXT, 155
Time function, 50
TIME( ), 50
TO FILE, 112, 123
TO PRINT, 51, 112, 123
TOTAL, 191
Totals, 105

Trim function, 49
TRIM(char string), 49
Tutorial Disk, 12
TXT, 80, 83, 84
Type, 25, 82
TYPE(expression), 51

U
Unary +,-, 45
UPDATE, 190
Upper case function, 49
UPPER(), 184
UPPER(char string), 49
USE, 27, 38, 62, 80, 84
   with ALIAS, 175
   with INDEX parameter, 64
USING, 162
Utilities Disk, 12

V
VAL(char string), 50

W
WAIT, 133, 154
What is command, 44
Width, 25
WordStar, 83
Work area, 174

Y
YEAR(date variable), 51

Z
ZAP, 92

Notes

Notes

Notes

Notes

Notes

Notes

Notes

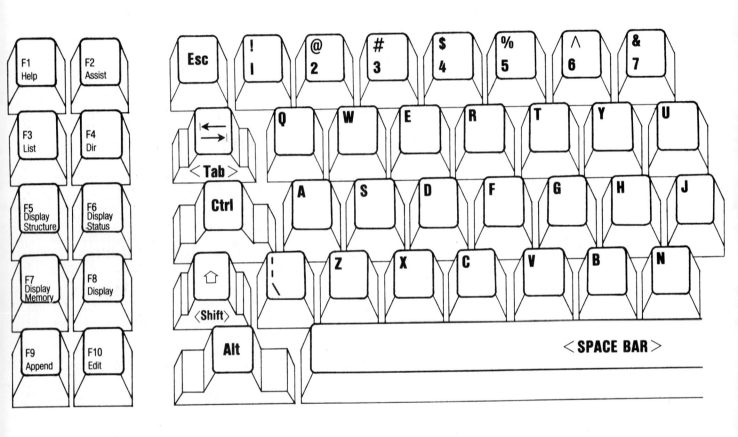

dBASE III KEYBOARD

F1	Help;
F2	Assist;
F3	List;
F4	Dir;
F5	Display Structure;
F6	Display Status;
F7	Display Memory;
F8	Display;
F9	Append;
F10	Edit;

The commands assigned to the function keys may be changed—see Unit 7.

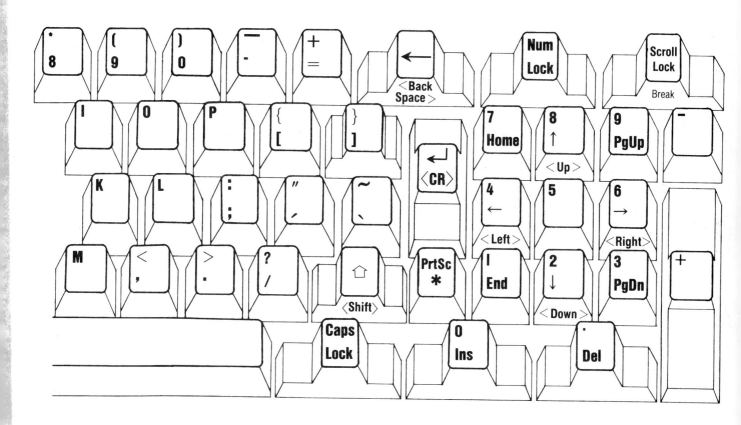

IBM PC™ Abbreviations

Esc—Escape Key

Ctrl—Control Key

Alt—Alternate Key

Num Lock—Number Lock Key

Pg Up—Page Up Key

PrtSc—Print Screen Key

Pg Dn—Page Down Key

Ins— Insert Character Key

Del— Delete Character Key

Quick Reference

These are the commands that you will use most often once you finish this manual. They are listed here for convenient reference.

Command	Purpose
CREATE	to specify the structure of a new file
USE	to open a file for input or output
APPEND	to add data to the end of a file
QUIT	to exit dBASE and save all work
DISPLAY	to show the contents of one or more records
LIST	to show the contents of one or more records
EDIT	to change the contents of a record
?	to display the value of an expression
INDEX	to build a file of pointers
REINDEX	to rebuild an index
FIND	to move cell pointer to the record with specified index key
LOCATE ... CONTINUE	to move cell pointer to records with specified contents
COUNT	to count occurrences
SUM	to sum numeric data
AVERAGE	to average numeric data*
COPY	to duplicate all or part of a file
DISPLAY STATUS	to show the current operating environment
DIR	to list files on a disk**
SET DEFAULT TO ...	to change default disk
SET PRINTER ON/OFF	to toggle printer on and off
REPLACE	to change the contents of a field
DELETE	to mark a record as deleted
RECALL	to remove the deleted mark
PACK	to remove deleted records from the data file
DISPLAY STRUCTURE	to show the structure of a data file
MODIFY STRUCTURE	to change the structure of a data file
MODIFY REPORT	to create or change a report format file*
REPORT FORM	to produce a report***
MODIFY LABEL	to create or change a label format file*
LABEL FORM	to produce labels*

---

* Not available in dBASE II

** In dBASE II, the command is DISPLAY FILES

*** In dBASE II, this command is also used to create the report format file